Finding Your Edge

Actionable Tactics to Beat Online Competitors

(Even the Big Ones)

Dominate Your Niche, Outsmart the Giants, and Build a Thriving Online Business

Created By: Julia James

About the Author: Julia James

Julia James is a seasoned strategist with fifteen years navigating the dynamic confluence of online business development and Search Engine Optimization (SEO). Her journey hasn't been confined to theory; she has spent over a decade in the trenches, building, advising, and scaling digital ventures across diverse industries. This hands-on experience has provided her with an intimate understanding of the challenges and opportunities inherent in today's hyper-competitive online marketplace, particularly for businesses striving to stand out against larger, more established players.

Having witnessed firsthand the escalating intensity of digital competition, Julia developed a passion for uncovering the specific strategies that allow smaller, more agile businesses to not only survive but actively thrive. She recognized early on that while resources matter, strategic positioning, deep customer understanding, and technical savvy – especially in the realm of SEO – could act as powerful equalizers.

Julia possesses a profound understanding of SEO, viewing it not merely as a technical checklist, but as a critical lever for visibility, credibility, and targeted customer acquisition. She excels at demystifying complex SEO concepts and translating them into actionable tactics that drive real-world results, helping businesses cut through the noise and connect with their ideal audience organically.

In **Finding Your Edge**, Julia distills her hard-won insights and proven methodologies into a pragmatic blend of strategic foresight and tactical execution. She believes passionately that success online isn't solely reserved for those with the deepest pockets, but for those who are smartest, fastest, and most adept at carving out and defending their unique space. Her approach emphasizes actionable steps, data-driven decisions, and leveraging the inherent advantages of agility and focus.

Julia's mission is to empower entrepreneurs and business leaders with the knowledge and confidence to move beyond mere survival, enabling them to find their distinct edge, compete effectively against any competitor (regardless of size), and build sustainable, profitable online businesses.

The Table of Contents

Introduction:

Why This Book Matters

Imagine David facing Goliath – except this isn't a dusty biblical tale. It's your everyday reality in the online business arena. You, the agile, driven entrepreneur, staring up at the Goliaths of your industry – the mega-corporations with seemingly limitless resources, the established brands that have dominated for decades. Perhaps you've launched your online store, meticulously crafted your service offerings, or poured your creativity into your digital product. Then, you look around. And *they* are everywhere. Their marketing budgets dwarf yours, their websites boast armies of developers, and their brand recognition feels impenetrable.

Sound familiar? You're not alone. The internet, once hailed as the great democratizer, can sometimes feel like a digital Colosseum, where only the titans clash, leaving smaller players struggling in the shadows. You might be asking yourself: "How can *I* possibly compete? Is there any point in even trying?"

Here's the invigorating truth: **Absolutely, yes. Not only can you compete, but you can win.** You don't need to outspend them, out-muscle them, or become a corporate behemoth yourself. What you *do* need is **an edge**. And that edge isn't about size, it's about **smart strategy, focused execution, and a deep understanding of the evolving digital landscape.**

This book, *Finding Your Edge: Actionable Tactics to Beat Online Competitors (Even the Big Ones)*, is your field manual for precisely that. Forget the defeatist narratives. We're not here to tell you to find a deserted island in the vast ocean of online business. We're here to equip you with the tools, tactics, and mindset to navigate the competitive currents, carve out your territory, and thrive – even when surrounded by digital giants.

The online business battlefield: Why is competition fiercer than ever

Let's not sugarcoat it. The digital marketplace is intensely competitive. The barriers to entry have plummeted. Anyone with a laptop and an internet connection can launch an online business, and millions have. This democratization is incredible, creating unparalleled opportunities, but it also means the noise level is deafening.

Customers are bombarded with choices. Attention spans are shorter than ever. Loyalty is fleeting. Big brands leverage their established power, vast datasets, and deep pockets to dominate search results, social media feeds, and customer mindshare. Small businesses often feel squeezed, fighting for scraps, struggling to gain visibility, let alone profitability.

But this hyper-competitive environment isn't inherently negative. It's a dynamic ecosystem. It signifies a robust, active market – a market where demand *exists*. The challenge isn't the *presence* of competition; it's the *strategy* you employ to differentiate yourself and capture your share of that demand.

The hidden advantages of being the "underdog"

Here's the critical shift in perspective: being the "underdog," the smaller, more agile player, is not a weakness. It's your **secret weapon**. Big companies, while powerful, are often slow, bureaucratic, and disconnect from the evolving needs of individual customers. They are like lumbering battleships, difficult to maneuver quickly. You, on the other hand, are a speedboat – nimble, responsive, and able to change direction on a dime.

This book will show you how to exploit these inherent advantages. How to be faster, more personal, more innovative, and more deeply connected to your niche audience than any corporate giant could ever hope to be. We'll delve into:

- **Agility:** You can adapt to market changes and customer feedback at lightning speed, while big companies take months or years to pivot.

- **Personalization:** You can offer truly personalized experiences and build genuine relationships with customers, something large, impersonal corporations struggle to replicate on a scale.

- **Niche Focus:** You can laser-focus on a specific, profitable niche, becoming the undisputed expert, while giants are often spread thin across multiple markets.

- **Innovation:** You can be more daring, experimental, and innovative, unburdened by layers of bureaucracy and risk aversion.

- **Community Building:** You can foster a tight-knit community around your brand, turning customers into loyal advocates, something corporate marketing machines can't manufacture authentically.

How this book will help you carve out your competitive edge

Finding Your Edge is not about wishful thinking or vague motivational speeches. It's a practical, hands-on guide packed with **actionable tactics** you can implement immediately to start outperforming your competitors – even the big ones.

We will take a step-by-step approach, covering:

- **Understanding the Competitive Landscape:** Analyzing your rivals, identifying their weaknesses, and pinpointing market gaps.

- **Building Your Unique Edge:** Crafting a powerful USP, mastering brand positioning, and niching down for maximum impact.

- **Tactical Marketing Strategies:** Outsmarting competitors with smarter SEO, content marketing, social media engagement, and guerrilla marketing techniques – all on a budget that works for *you*.

- **Leveraging Speed and Innovation:** Exploiting your agility to move faster, iterate quicker, and adopt new technologies before the giants catch on.

- **Cultivating Customer Loyalty:** Building a brand that customers trust, love, and actively advocate for, creating a powerful, sustainable competitive moat.

- **Scaling for Long-Term Success:** Expanding your reach without losing the unique edge that made you successful in the first place.

Throughout this book, you'll find:

- **Real-world examples and case studies** to illustrate key principles and inspire action.

- **Step-by-step instructions and templates** to implement strategies immediately.

- **Self-reflection questions** to personalize the learning and apply it directly to *your* business.

- **Actionable checklists** to keep you on track and ensure you're implementing each tactic effectively.

Our tone will be encouraging and supportive, recognizing the challenges you face, but always emphasizing the immense potential that lies within your reach. This isn't about overnight miracles; it's about consistent, strategic effort that compounds over time, building a business that not only survives but thrives in the competitive online arena.

Are you ready to find your edge and start outmaneuvering the giants? Let's begin.

Part 1

The Reality of Competing Online

Chapter 1: Why Small Businesses Can Win

The narrative often goes like this: In the cutthroat world of online business, only the biggest, wealthiest, and most established companies truly succeed. Smaller businesses are destined to be crushed, outspent, and ultimately, irrelevant. This is a seductive, fear-inducing story, but it's profoundly **false**. It ignores the inherent strengths of smaller, more agile enterprises and the evolving dynamics of the modern marketplace.

Debunking the myth of corporate invincibility

Let's dismantle this myth of corporate invincibility piece by piece. While large corporations possess undeniable advantages in terms of resources and scale, they also carry significant **inherent weaknesses**:

- **Bureaucracy and Slow Decision-Making:** Large companies are often plagued by layers of management, complex approval processes, and internal politics. Decision-making becomes agonizingly slow. By the time a big company identifies a trend and decides to act on it, a smaller, nimbler business can have already capitalized on it and moved on to the next opportunity.

Think of it like turning a massive cruise ship versus a speedboat.

- **Lack of Personalization and Customer Connection:** Corporations strive for efficiency and standardization. Customer service often becomes impersonal, automated, and frustrating. Marketing messages are typically generic, broad brushstrokes designed to appeal to the widest possible audience, often failing to resonate deeply with anyone. This creates a vast opportunity for smaller businesses to offer genuinely personalized experiences and forge authentic human connections.

- **Risk Aversion and Stifled Innovation:** Large companies are often inherently risk averse. They protect their existing revenue streams and established brands, hesitant to disrupt themselves or embrace truly radical innovation. Smaller businesses, with less to lose, can afford to be bolder, more experimental, and more willing to try unconventional approaches. They can be the true innovators, driving market change.

- **Disconnect from Niche Audiences:** Giants are often forced to target the broadest possible demographics to justify their massive scale. They can't

14

afford to deeply cater to highly specific, niche audiences. This leaves vast swathes of underserved customers craving more specialized solutions, personalized experiences, and brands that truly understand their unique needs and values. This is fertile ground for niche-focused small businesses to thrive.

- **Vulnerability to Disruption:** History is littered with examples of massive corporations being toppled by smaller, more agile disruptors. Think of Netflix disrupting Blockbuster, or digital-first brands challenging established retail giants. These disruptions often arise because the larger, more established players are too slow, too complacent, and too tied to their legacy models to adapt quickly enough.

How smaller businesses have outmaneuvered giants (real-world examples)

Let's move beyond theory and examine real-world examples of smaller businesses not just surviving, but actively outmaneuvering industry giants:

- **Dollar Shave Club vs. Gillette:** Gillette dominated the razor market for decades. Enter Dollar Shave Club, a startup with a humorous, irreverent brand and a subscription-based model. They offered convenience, affordability, and a personality that resonated with younger consumers. Gillette, the behemoth, was slow to respond, clinging to its traditional retail distribution model. Dollar Shave Club, the agile upstart, captured significant market share and was eventually acquired by Unilever for a billion dollars.

Lesson: Disruption can come from a superior customer experience and a brand that connects emotionally, even in a seemingly commoditized market.

- **Warby Parker vs. Luxottica:** Luxottica controlled a massive share of the eyewear market through brands like Ray-Ban and Oakley, often dictating prices and limiting consumer choice. Warby Parker, an online-first eyewear company, emerged offering stylish, high-quality glasses at affordable prices, sold directly to consumers online. They emphasized social impact, transparent pricing, and a modern brand aesthetic. Warby Parker directly challenged Luxottica's control, demonstrating that a direct-to-consumer model, coupled with strong branding and value, could disrupt a highly concentrated industry. **Lesson:** Transparency, value pricing, and a strong online presence can dismantle established monopolies.

- **Numerous Independent Craft Breweries vs. Anheuser-Busch InBev:** For years, the beer market was dominated by a few mega-breweries producing mass-market lagers. However, a craft beer revolution erupted, fueled by smaller, independent breweries focused on quality, unique flavors, and local community. Consumers increasingly sought out these craft options, valuing authenticity and variety. While giants like Anheuser-Busch InBev still hold a large market share, craft breweries have carved out a substantial and growing segment, proving that passion, quality, and niche appeal can triumph over sheer scale. **Lesson:** Focus on quality, craftsmanship, and niche appeal to capture a dedicated customer base willing to pay a premium for something unique.

These examples share common threads:

- **Niche Focus:** They often targeted specific underserved niches or customer segments.

- **Superior Customer Experience:** They offered better service, convenience, personalization, or a more compelling brand experience.

- **Agility and Speed:** They were faster to adapt, innovate, and respond to changing market demands.

- **Strong Branding and Storytelling:** They built brands that resonated emotionally with their target audiences, going beyond just product features.

The agility and personalization advantage

The core advantage of smaller online businesses boils down to **agility** and **personalization**. These are superpowers that big companies simply can't replicate effectively.

- **Agility in Action:**

  - **Rapid Product Iteration:** You can quickly test new product features, designs, or service offerings based on immediate customer feedback, making changes within days or weeks. Large companies often have product development cycles measured in years.

  - **Nimble Marketing Campaigns:** You can launch and adjust

marketing campaigns in real-time, reacting to trends, competitor moves, or social media buzz with speed and precision.

- o **Fast Response to Market Shifts:** When market conditions change (economic downturn, emerging technologies, new consumer preferences), you can pivot your strategy, adjust your offerings, and reposition your business with far greater speed and flexibility.

- **Personalization Power:**

  - o **Truly Personalized Customer Service:** You can offer one-on-one support, build personal relationships with key customers, and go the extra mile in ways that corporate scripts and automated systems simply can't match.

  - o **Tailored Product Recommendations:** You can leverage customer data (purchase history, browsing behavior, direct interactions) to provide highly relevant and personalized product suggestions, creating a "concierge" shopping experience.

- **Authentic Brand Voice and Connection:** You can communicate with a genuine, human voice that reflects your brand's personality and values, building a strong emotional connection with your audience that feels authentic, not manufactured.

- **Community Building:** You can foster a tight-knit community around your brand, engaging in direct conversations, soliciting feedback, and creating a sense of belonging that transcends transactional interactions.

Self-Reflection Questions:

- In what specific ways are my larger competitors slow or bureaucratic in my industry? How can I exploit these weaknesses?

- Where are my big competitors failing to offer personalized experiences or build genuine customer connections?

- What are some areas where I can be more agile, experimental, or innovative compared to the established players?

- How can I better leverage my smaller size to offer superior customer service and build stronger relationships?

- What niche or underserved customer segment could I focus on that larger companies are overlooking?

The myth of corporate invincibility is just that – a myth. Smaller online businesses, armed with agility, personalization, and strategic thinking, are not just survivors in the digital jungle; they are often the most adaptable, innovative, and ultimately, the most successful. It's time to shed the underdog mentality and embrace your inherent strengths. The giants may be big, but you can be smarter, faster, and far more connected to the customers who matter most.

Chapter 2: Mastering Competitive Analysis

You can't outmaneuver an opponent if you don't understand them. Competitive analysis isn't about copying what your rivals do – it's about dissecting their strategies, identifying their strengths and, crucially, their **weaknesses**, and uncovering the gaps they leave in the market that *you* can exploit. Think of it as reconnaissance – gathering intelligence before you launch your strategic campaign. This isn't about industrial espionage; it's about ethical, intelligent observation and data-driven insight.

How to dissect your competitors' strengths and weaknesses

Competitive analysis should be a systematic, multi-faceted process. Don't rely on gut feelings or anecdotal observations. Employ a structured approach:

1. **Identify Your Key Competitors:** Start by listing your top 3-5 *direct* competitors – those offering similar products or services to the same target audience. Then, consider *indirect* competitors – those who address the same customer needs but in different ways. Don't just focus on the biggest names; include smaller, emerging players as well. Cast a wide net initially, then prioritize based on

relevance and perceived threat/opportunity.

2. **Website and Online Presence Audit:** This is your first and most accessible source of intelligence. Scrutinize their websites from a customer's perspective:

   o **User Experience (UX):** Is their website easy to navigate? Is it mobile-friendly? How fast does it load? Is the design modern and professional? Where are the friction points? (Slow loading, confusing navigation, etc.)

   o **Product/Service Offering:** What exactly do they sell? How is it priced? What are the key features and benefits they emphasize? What guarantees or warranties do they offer? Are there gaps in their product line?

   o **Content Strategy:** Do they have a blog? What topics do they cover? How frequently do they publish? Is their content high-quality, engaging, and valuable? What content formats do they use (blog posts, videos, infographics, podcasts)?

- SEO Strategy (Visible On-Page Elements): Analyze their website's structure, keyword usage in titles and descriptions, header tags, and internal linking. Look at their URL structure. (We'll delve into deeper SEO analysis later in this chapter).

- Social Media Presence: Which platforms are they active on? What type of content do they post? How often do they engage with their audience? What is their social media tone and personality? What are their follower counts and engagement levels (likes, comments, shares)?

- Customer Service and Support: Look for clues about their customer service approach. Do they offer live chat, phone support, email support? Check their FAQs and knowledge base. Read customer reviews (both positive and negative) to gauge customer satisfaction levels.

3. Marketing and Sales Analysis: Go beyond their website and observe their marketing activities:

- **Email Marketing:** Sign up for their email list. Analyze the frequency, content, and value of their emails. Are they primarily promotional, or do they offer valuable content and relationship-building communication?

- **Paid Advertising:** Observe their online ads (social media, search engine ads, display ads). What keywords are they targeting? What is their ad copy like? What offers or promotions do they run? (Tools like SpyFu or SEMrush can help with paid ad analysis).

- **Sales Funnels:** If possible, try to go through their sales process (e.g., from landing page to checkout). How smooth is the funnel? Are there any points where customers might drop off? What conversion optimization tactics do they employ?

- **Pricing Strategy:** Analyze their pricing in detail. Are they positioning themselves as the cheapest, the most premium, or somewhere in between? What pricing models do they use (subscription, one-time purchase, tiered pricing)? How does their pricing compare to yours and other competitors?

- o **Promotional Offers and Discounts:** Track their seasonal promotions, discounts, and special offers. How frequently do they run sales? What types of discounts do they offer?

4. **Customer Reviews and Sentiment Analysis:** Customer reviews are goldmines of information about competitor strengths and weaknesses:

- o **Read Reviews Extensively:** Analyze reviews on platforms like Google My Business, Yelp, Amazon, product review sites, and social media. Look for recurring themes, both positive and negative.

- o **Identify Strengths:** What aspects do customers consistently praise? (e.g., "fast shipping," "excellent customer service," "high-quality product"). These are areas where your competitors excel.

- o **Uncover Weaknesses:** What are the common complaints? (e.g., "slow response times," "poor website navigation," "products break easily"). These are your potential opportunities – areas where you can outperform them.

- o **Sentiment Analysis Tools (Optional):** For larger-scale analysis, you can use sentiment analysis tools to automatically analyze customer reviews and social media mentions to gauge overall customer sentiment and identify key themes.

5. **SWOT Analysis (Strengths, Weaknesses, Opportunities, Threats):** Summarize your findings in a structured SWOT analysis for each major competitor. This framework helps you organize your intelligence and identify key strategic implications:

- o **Strengths:** What are they doing exceptionally well? Where do they have a clear advantage? (e.g., strong brand recognition, large marketing budget, established distribution network).

- o **Weaknesses:** Where are they vulnerable? What are they doing poorly or neglecting? (e.g., slow customer service, outdated website, generic marketing messages, high prices).

- **Opportunities:** Based on their weaknesses, what opportunities exist for *you* to gain a competitive edge? (e.g., offer faster shipping, provide more personalized support, create more engaging content, target a specific niche they are ignoring).

- **Threats:** What aspects of their business could potentially threaten *your* success? (e.g., aggressive pricing strategies, new product launches, acquisition of smaller competitors).

Essential tools for spying (ethically) on competitors (SEMrush, Ahrefs, etc.)

While manual analysis is crucial, several powerful online tools can significantly streamline and deepen your competitive intelligence gathering (always use these tools ethically and within their terms of service):

- **SEMrush:** A comprehensive suite of SEO and competitive analysis tools. Key features for competitive research:

  - **Competitor Keyword Analysis:** See what keywords your

competitors are ranking for in organic search, including traffic volume and keyword difficulty.

o **Backlink Analysis:** Analyze your competitors' backlink profiles – where are they getting links from? This can uncover link-building opportunities for you.

o **Advertising Research:** See your competitors' paid search ads, keywords they bid on, and estimated ad spend.

o **Traffic Analytics:** Estimate your competitors' website traffic, traffic sources, and audience demographics.

o **Content Gap Analysis:** Identify content topics where your competitors rank well but you don't, revealing content opportunities.
https://www.semrush.com/

- **Ahrefs:** Another leading SEO and competitive analysis platform, similar to SEMrush, often praised for its backlink analysis capabilities. Key competitive features:

- **Site Explorer:** Analyze any website's backlink profile, organic keywords, and estimated traffic.

- **Content Explorer:** Discover top-performing content on any topic and analyze competitor content strategies.

- **Keyword Explorer:** Research keyword difficulty, search volume, and keyword ideas.

- **Competitor Analysis Tools:** Compare your website's SEO metrics with competitors and identify areas for improvement. https://ahrefs.com/

- **SpyFu:** Primarily focused on competitor keyword research, especially for paid advertising. Key features for competition:

  - **Keyword Research:** Discover keywords your competitors are buying in Google Ads and their organic rankings.

  - **Competitor Ad History:** See historical ad campaigns run by your competitors.

  - **SEO Research:** Analyze competitors' organic rankings,

backlinks, and content.
https://www.spyfu.com/

- **BuiltWith:** Reveals the technologies used to build any website – from content management systems (CMS) to e-commerce platforms, analytics tools, and widgets. Useful for understanding your competitors' technical infrastructure. https://builtwith.com/

- **Similarweb:** Provides website traffic statistics, traffic sources, audience demographics, and competitor comparisons. Useful for benchmarking your website performance against rivals and understanding overall market share. https://www.similarweb.com/

Finding market gaps they ignore

The ultimate goal of competitive analysis is to uncover **market gaps** – underserved customer needs, unmet desires, or neglected segments that your competitors are overlooking. These gaps are your goldmine, your opportunity to differentiate and dominate. Gaps can exist in several forms:

- **Product/Service Gaps:** Are there features, functionalities, or service aspects that your competitors are missing or underperforming on? Could you offer a more comprehensive solution, a higher-quality product, or a more specialized service?

- **Price Gaps:** Are your competitors primarily targeting the high-end or low-end of the market? Is there a segment seeking a mid-range option, a more affordable solution, or a premium alternative?

- **Customer Service Gaps:** Are your competitors known for poor customer support, slow response times, or impersonal interactions? Could you differentiate by providing exceptional, proactive, and highly personalized customer service?

- **Content and Information Gaps:** Is there valuable information, educational content, or resources that your competitors are not providing in your niche? Could you become the go-to source of expertise and thought leadership by filling these content gaps?

- **Niche Audience Gaps:** Are your competitors broadly targeting large demographics, neglecting more specific, niche audiences with unique needs and preferences? Could you specialize in serving a particular micro-niche, offering highly tailored solutions?

- **Geographical Gaps (For Local or Regional Businesses):** Are your competitors primarily focused on national or international markets, neglecting local or regional opportunities? Could you dominate your local market by offering specialized local services or content?

- **Value Gaps:** Are your competitors failing to connect with customers on an emotional or values-based level? Could you build a brand that resonates with specific values, beliefs, or lifestyles that your competitors are ignoring?

Self-Reflection Questions:

- Who are my top 3-5 direct competitors and 2-3 indirect competitors?

- What are the most impressive strengths of my main competitors? What can I learn from them?

- What are the most glaring weaknesses of my main competitors? How can I capitalize on these?

- What market gaps am I currently aware of in my industry? Are there any I am overlooking?

- Which competitor analysis tools could be most valuable for my business to gain deeper insights?

Competitive analysis is not a one-time task; it's an ongoing process. The market is dynamic, competitors evolve, and new players emerge. Make competitive analysis a regular part of your business strategy – continuously monitoring, analyzing, and adapting. By understanding your competitors' landscape deeply, you position yourself not just to compete, but to strategically outmaneuver them, finding the gaps where you can truly excel and build your unassailable edge.

Part 2

Finding & Building Your Unique Competitive Edge

Chapter 3: The Power of Micro-Niching

Imagine trying to be the loudest voice in a stadium filled with roaring crowds. It's exhausting, expensive, and ultimately ineffective. Yet, this is precisely what many online businesses attempt when they target broad, saturated markets dominated by established giants. They spread their resources thin, their message gets diluted, and they struggle to gain traction against competitors with far greater reach and deeper pockets.

There's a smarter way. A way to sidestep the deafening roar and become the most resonant voice in a smaller, more receptive room. This is the power of **micro-niching**: the strategic decision to focus your efforts on a very specific, well-defined segment of a larger market. It might seem counterintuitive – shrinking your potential audience – but for smaller businesses aiming to compete against giants, it's often the most effective path to dominance and profitability.

Why going broad is a death sentence for small players

Trying to be everything to everyone when you're a smaller player is a recipe for mediocrity, or worse, failure. Here's why a broad approach is often fatal:

1. **Direct Collision with Giants:** Targeting a broad market puts you in direct, head-to-head competition with the largest players who have massive advantages in brand recognition, marketing spend, and operational scale. You simply can't out-muscle them on their home turf.

2. **Diluted Resources:** As a smaller business, your resources (time, money, manpower) are finite. Spreading them across a vast market means you can't make a significant impact anywhere. Your marketing becomes less targeted, your product development less focused, and your customer service less personalized.

3. **Generic Messaging:** To appeal to a broad audience, your marketing message inevitably becomes more generic. It lacks the specificity and relevance needed to truly resonate with any particular group, making it easy for potential customers to ignore you amidst the noise.

4. **Inability to Build Deep Expertise:** It's impossible to be the absolute best at everything. A broad focus prevents you from developing the deep expertise and specialized knowledge required to become the undisputed leader in any

specific area. You become a jack-of-all-trades, master of none.

5. **Price Sensitivity:** In broad markets, competition often devolves into a price war. Without a clear differentiator, customers default to the cheapest option, a game smaller business can rarely win against giants with economies of scale.

How to carve out and dominate a micro-niche

Micro-niching isn't just about choosing a smaller market; it's about identifying a segment with specific needs, preferences, or problems that are currently underserved by the larger players. It's about becoming the big fish in a small, profitable pond.

Identifying Potential Micro-Niches:

- **Drill Down Within Your Existing Market:** Start with your broad industry (e.g., "pet supplies") and progressively narrow your focus.

  - *Demographics:* "Pet supplies for elderly dog owners."

  - *Psychographics/Values:* "Pet supplies for eco-conscious millennials."

- Specific Problem: "Pet supplies for dogs with severe skin allergies."

- Specific Product Type: "Subscription boxes featuring only natural, limited-ingredient dog treats."

- Geographic Focus (if applicable): "Handmade dog accessories sourced from local artisans in [Specific Region]."

- **Analyze Competitor Weaknesses (From Chapter 2):** Where are the giants falling short? Are there customer segments they ignore? Are there specific pain points their broad solutions don't adequately address? Their blind spots are your opportunities.

- **Listen Intently to Your Target Audience:** Engage in online forums (like Reddit subs related to your industry), Facebook groups, social media comment sections, and analyze customer reviews (yours and competitors'). What specific frustrations, unmet needs, or niche interests keep surfacing? What language do they use to describe their problems?

- **Explore Intersections of Your Skills and Passions:** Combine your unique expertise, experience, and interests. Perhaps your background in graphic design *and* your love for tabletop gaming could lead to a niche in designing custom character sheets or game accessories.

- **Identify "Long-Tail" Keywords:** Use SEO tools (SEMrush, Ahrefs) to find highly specific, lower-volume search terms related to your industry. These "long-tail" keywords often indicate niche interests and underserved needs (e.g., "best hiking gear for small dogs" vs. "dog gear"). Chapter 6 will delve deeper into this.

- **Look for Emerging Trends or Subcultures:** Are there new trends, technologies, or passionate subcultures developing within your broader market? Being an early provider for these emerging niches can establish you as a leader.

Validating Your Micro-Niche:

Once you have potential micro-niche ideas, validate their viability:

- **Sufficient Size & Purchasing Power:** Is the niche large enough to sustain your business? Do the members of this niche have the willingness and ability to pay for your solution? (It doesn't need to be massive, just profitable for *you*).

- **Identifiable & Reachable:** Can you easily identify and reach the members of this niche through specific marketing channels (e.g., dedicated online communities, specific hashtags, targeted advertising)?

- **Genuine Need or Passion:** Does this niche have a significant pain point you can solve or a strong passion you can cater to? The stronger the need or passion, the more likely they are to seek out specialized solutions.

- **Long-Term Potential:** Is this niche likely to persist or grow, or is it based on a fleeting fad?

- **Underserved by Competitors:** Critically assess if larger competitors are truly ignoring or poorly serving this specific niche. Is there a genuine gap you can fill?

Dominating Your Micro-Niche:

- **Become the Expert:** Immerse yourself in the niche. Understand their unique language, challenges, desires, and culture. Create content, products, and services that speak *directly* to them. Position yourself as the go-to authority.

- **Tailor Everything:** Customize your products, services, marketing messages, website experience, and customer support specifically for the needs and preferences of your micro-niche. Generic approaches won't cut it.

- **Build Community:** Foster a sense of belonging among your niche audience. Create dedicated spaces for them to connect (Facebook groups, forums), share user-generated content, and engage deeply with your brand.

- **Hyper-Targeted Marketing:** Focus your marketing efforts solely on the channels where your micro-niche congregates. This leads to higher conversion rates and a better return on investment compared to broad marketing campaigns.

- **Deliver Exceptional Value:** Because you're focused, you can often provide superior quality, deeper expertise, or more personalized service within your niche than any generalist competitor could. Exceed their expectations.

Case studies of businesses that became #1 in a small but profitable space

(Conceptual examples illustrating the principle)

- **"Vintage Synth Restorers":** Instead of competing in the broad market of musical instrument sales, this online business focused *only* on restoring and selling rare, vintage synthesizers from the 1970s and 80s.

  - *Micro-Niche:* Musicians and collectors specifically seeking authentic, working vintage synthesizers, often frustrated by the poor condition or lack of expertise found in general music stores.

  - *Dominance Strategy:* Became the ultimate experts in sourcing, repairing, and authenticating these specific instruments. Built a reputation for meticulous restoration and deep knowledge. Created highly detailed content (videos, articles) about vintage synth history and maintenance. Built a community forum for vintage synth enthusiasts. They charged premium prices due to their unique expertise and inventory.

- **"Keto Bakers Box":** Rather than competing with countless general subscription boxes, this company niched down *exclusively* to curated boxes of low-carb, keto-friendly baking ingredients and recipes.

  - *Micro-Niche:* Individuals strictly following a ketogenic diet who love baking but struggle to find compliant ingredients or inspiring recipes easily.

  - *Dominance Strategy:* Focused solely on sourcing high-quality, verified keto ingredients. Developed unique, tested keto baking recipes. Created content specifically addressing the challenges of keto baking. Built a community around sharing keto baking successes and tips. Became the trusted source for this specific dietary need.

- **"Left-Handed Guitar Hub":** This online retailer ignored the massive right-handed guitar market and focused *only* on serving left-handed guitar players.

- *Micro-Niche:* Left-handed guitarists often frustrated by the limited selection, lack of expertise, and higher prices typically found in general guitar stores.

- *Dominance Strategy:* Offered the widest possible selection of left-handed guitars across various brands and price points. Provided expert advice specifically for left-handed players (setup, technique). Created content addressing the unique challenges and joys of being a lefty guitarist. Built a reputation as the supportive, go-to destination for this underserved group.

These businesses didn't try to conquer the world. They chose a specific corner, understood it deeply, served it exceptionally well, and became indispensable to that audience.

Self-Reflection Questions:

- Is my current target market too broad? Am I trying to be everything to everyone?

- What specific sub-groups exist within my broader market? Which ones seem most underserved or passionate?

- What unique problems or frustrations do these sub-groups face that larger competitors might be ignoring?

- How could I tailor my products, services, or marketing to *specifically* address the needs of one chosen micro-niche?

- What steps can I take this week to research and validate a potential micro-niche for my business?

Micro-niching is not about thinking small; it's about thinking **smart**. It's about strategically choosing your battlefield, focusing your firepower, and becoming the indispensable leader within a defined territory. For the agile online business facing down giants, it's often the clearest path to finding – and dominating – your edge.

Chapter 4: Positioning Like a Pro

You've identified your micro-niche (Chapter 3). You know *who* you want to serve. Now comes the crucial question: **Why should they choose you?** In a marketplace saturated with options, simply existing in a niche isn't enough. You need to consciously shape how your target audience perceives your brand relative to the competition. This deliberate act of carving out a distinct and desirable space in the customer's mind is **positioning**.

Effective positioning is your shield and sword against larger competitors. It communicates your unique value proposition so clearly and compellingly that price becomes less of a factor, and the perceived risk of choosing a smaller player diminishes. It's about making your brand the obvious, irresistible choice for your specific audience.

Crafting an irresistible Unique Selling Proposition (USP)

At the heart of powerful positioning lies your Unique Selling Proposition (USP). This isn't just a catchy slogan; it's the core, concise articulation of **what makes you different and uniquely valuable to your target customer.** It answers the fundamental question: "Why should I buy from you rather than anyone else, especially the big, established brands?"

A truly effective USP in a competitive market needs to be:

1. **Unique:** It must highlight something genuinely distinct about your offering that competitors cannot easily claim or replicate. This could be a specific feature, a unique process, a targeted benefit, superior service, a particular ingredient, or a strong brand ethos.

2. **Selling:** It must resonate with a strong customer need or desire. Your uniqueness needs to *matter* to your target audience, solving a significant problem or fulfilling a key aspiration better than alternatives.

3. **Proposition:** It must be a clear, concise, and easily understandable statement or promise. Avoid jargon or vague claims. It should be memorable and easily communicable.

4. **Provable:** You must be able to consistently deliver on the promise embedded in your USP. Empty claims erode trust faster than anything else.

Why is a Sharp USP Critical Against Big Competitors?

Large companies often struggle with pinpoint USPs. Their need to appeal broadly can lead to diluted messaging. They might rely on brand recognition or general claims of "quality" or "value." This creates an opening for you. A sharp, specific USP allows you to:

- **Cut Through the Noise:** A specific promise stands out against generic corporate messaging.

- **Attract Ideal Customers:** It acts like a magnet, drawing in the exact customers who value what you uniquely offer and repelling those who aren't a good fit.

- **Justify Premium Pricing (Potentially):** If your USP addresses a high value need or offers a unique benefit, customers may be willing to pay more compared to generic alternatives.

- **Focus Your Efforts:** Your USP becomes the guiding principle for your marketing, product development, and customer service, ensuring consistency and reinforcing your edge.

Framework for Crafting Your USP:

Developing a powerful USP requires introspection, customer empathy, and competitive awareness. Follow these steps:

1. **Revisit Your Strengths & Passions:** What does your business do exceptionally well? What unique skills, knowledge, resources, or values do you possess? What are you genuinely passionate about delivering?

2. **Deep Dive into Your Micro-Niche's Needs (Chapter 3):** What are their biggest pain points, frustrations, desires, and aspirations related specifically to the problem you solve? Use their language. What outcomes are they *really* seeking?

3. **Analyze Competitor USPs (Stated or Implied - Chapter 2):** What promises are your competitors making? Where are their messages weak, generic, or failing to address the specific needs of *your* micro-niche? What ground can you claim that they haven't?

4. **Brainstorm Potential Differentiators:** Based on the above, list all possible ways you are, or could be, different. Think broadly: product features, service levels, speed, convenience, ingredients/materials, origin story, brand

values, specific expertise, guarantees, customer experience, community aspect.

5. **Identify the Sweet Spot:** Look for the intersection where your unique strengths align perfectly with a high-priority need of your micro-niche and represent a weakness or gap in your competitors' offerings. (Imagine a Venn diagram).

6. **Formulate Concise USP Statements:** Draft several potential USP statements based on the sweet spot identified. Use this template as a starting point:

   o "We help [Your Micro-Niche] achieve [Desired Outcome] by providing [Your Unique Offering/Method], unlike [Competitors] who [Competitor Weakness/Generic Approach]."

   o "For [Your Micro-Niche] who struggle with [Specific Pain Point], our [Product/Service] offers [Unique Benefit/Solution] through [Unique Feature/Process]."

7. **Refine and Test:** Make your statements clear, concise, benefit-driven, and memorable. Get feedback (ideally from potential customers in your niche). Does it resonate? Is it believable? Does it clearly differentiate you?

Examples of Strong vs. Weak USPs:

- **Weak (Generic):** "We sell high-quality coffee online." (Doesn't differentiate)

- **Strong (Niche/Benefit Focused):** "We deliver single-origin, shade-grown coffee, freshly roasted within 24 hours of shipping, exclusively for home espresso enthusiasts seeking peak crema and complex flavor profiles." (Unique process, specific niche, clear benefit)

- **Weak (Vague):** "Marketing services for small businesses." (Doesn't stand out)

- **Strong (Problem/Solution/Guarantee Focused):** "We guarantee a 50% increase in qualified leads within 90 days for B2B SaaS startups under $5M ARR using our proprietary content-driven SEO system, or you don't pay." (Specific niche, measurable outcome, unique guarantee, addresses risk)

- **Weak (Feature-Based):** "Our software has AI features." (Doesn't explain the benefit)

- **Strong (Benefit/Target User Focused):** "Our AI-powered scheduling software automatically finds the optimal meeting times for busy remote teams across multiple time zones, eliminating scheduling headaches and saving hours each week." (Clear benefit, specific user, solves pain point)

Your USP is not set in stone forever. As the market evolves, you may need to refine it. But having a strong, clear USP *now* is fundamental to effective positioning.

The psychology of brand differentiation

Positioning isn't just about *what* you say; it's about *how* it lands in the customer's psyche. Understanding basic psychological principles can help you differentiate your brand more effectively, making it stickier and more appealing than larger, more impersonal competitors.

- **The Halo Effect:** First impressions matter immensely. A professionally designed website, high-quality product photography, and clear, error-free communication create a positive "halo" that makes customers perceive everything else about your brand more favorably. Small businesses can often achieve a higher level of polish and attention to detail in their specific niche than giants managing vast portfolios.

- **Authority & Expertise:** Position yourself as the definitive expert within your micro-niche. Consistently share valuable, in-depth content (blogs, guides, webinars), showcase testimonials from recognized figures (if possible), and use professional certifications or credentials. People trust experts, especially when navigating complex choices. Big companies often have generic content; you can provide deep, niche-specific authority.

- **Social Proof:** Leverage testimonials, reviews, case studies, user-generated content, and "number of customers served" metrics prominently. When potential customers see that *others like them* trust and value your brand, it dramatically reduces perceived risk and builds credibility. Encourage reviews and make it easy for customers to share their positive experiences. While giants have scale, you can create more relatable, niche-specific social proof.

- **Liking Principle:** People prefer to buy from those they know, like, and trust. Humanize your brand! Share your founder's story, showcase your team (even if it's just you!), communicate with an authentic brand voice, and engage genuinely on social media. Smaller businesses can build rapport and personal connections in ways large corporations simply can't.

- **Scarcity & Urgency (Use Ethically):** Limited-time offers, small-batch production runs, exclusive access for loyal customers, or highlighting limited availability can increase perceived value and encourage faster decisions. Ensure scarcity is genuine to maintain trust. This can be easier to manage and communicate authentically for smaller operations.

- **Commitment & Consistency:** Encourage small initial commitments (e.g., signing up for a newsletter, downloading a free resource). Once someone makes a small commitment, they are psychologically more likely to make larger ones later to remain consistent with their initial action. Nurture leads effectively.

- **Loss Aversion:** Frame benefits in terms of what customers stand to *lose* by *not* choosing you (e.g., "Stop losing hours to scheduling chaos," "Don't miss out on peak coffee freshness"). People are often more motivated by avoiding losses than achieving gains.

By consciously weaving these psychological triggers into your branding, messaging, and customer interactions, you can create a more compelling and memorable brand identity that resonates deeply with your target audience.

How to make customers choose YOU over the big guys

Ultimately, positioning translates into tangible actions that influence customer choice. Here's how to tilt the scales in your favor:

1. **Hammer Your USP Everywhere:** Don't hide your unique value. Feature your USP prominently on your website homepage, in your social media bios, in your ad copy, in your email signature, and weave it into your content. Ensure every touchpoint reinforces *why* you are different and better *for them*.

2. **Emphasize Your Niche Focus:** Explicitly state who you serve. Use language like "Exclusively for..." or "Designed specifically for..." This signals expertise and relevance to your target audience, making generic competitors seem less suitable.

3. **Highlight Superior, Personalized Service:** If exceptional service is part of your edge, showcase it. Feature testimonials praising your support, offer multiple easy contact methods, promise fast response times, and empower your team (or yourself) to go above and

beyond. Contrast this with the often-frustrating experience of dealing with large company call centers.

4. **Showcase Your Agility & Responsiveness:** Subtly highlight how quickly you can adapt, implement feedback, or ship products compared to slower competitors. Frame this as a direct benefit to the customer (e.g., "Get the latest features faster," "We act on customer suggestions").

5. **Build and Leverage Your Community:** Feature your thriving community (if applicable). Show customers engaging, sharing successes, and supporting each other. This creates a powerful sense of belonging that big brand struggle to replicate authentically. Position your brand as the center of a passionate tribe.

6. **Offer Strong Guarantees:** Reduce the perceived risk of choosing a smaller player by offering robust satisfaction guarantees, longer warranty periods, or performance-based promises (like the SaaS example earlier). This demonstrates confidence in your offer.

7. **Focus on Value, Not Just Price:** While competitive pricing is important, don't make it your primary battleground

against giants. Focus on the *total value* you provide – the unique benefits, the expertise, the service, the community, the alignment with their values. Position yourself as the *smarter* choice, not just the cheaper one.

8. **Tell Your Story:** Share your brand's origin, mission, and values. People connect with authentic stories. Your unique journey can be a powerful differentiator that humanizes your brand and makes it more relatable than a faceless corporation.

Self-Reflection Questions:

- Is my current USP truly unique, specific, and compelling to my target niche? Can I articulate it in a single sentence?

- Where are the biggest psychological gaps in my competitors' branding (e.g., lack of personalization, weak authority signals)? How can I fill them?

- Which psychological principles (social proof, authority, liking, etc.) could I leverage more effectively in my marketing and website copy?

- Am I consistently communicating my USP across all customer touchpoints? Where could I reinforce it better?

- What specific actions can I take this month to make my brand the more attractive choice compared to larger competitors for my ideal customer?

Positioning isn't about deception; it's about clarity. It's about understanding your unique strengths, knowing your ideal customer intimately, and communicating your value so effectively that choosing you becomes the most logical, desirable, and satisfying decision they can make. Master this, and even the biggest competitors will struggle to dislodge you from your well-defended territory.

Chapter 5: Becoming a Customer Magnet

You've staked your claim in a micro-niche (Chapter 3) and crafted a compelling position (Chapter 4). Now, how do you ensure customers not only *choose* you initially but become fiercely loyal, returning again and again, and even singing your praises to others? The answer lies in transforming your customer interactions from mere transactions into memorable, positive experiences. In this area, smaller businesses possess a monumental advantage. While corporate giants often grapple with impersonal systems and bureaucratic red tape, you have the agility and inherent capacity to become a true **customer magnet**.

This chapter is about weaponizing exceptional customer service and engagement. It's about understanding the systemic flaws in how many large corporations handle customer relationships and strategically exploiting those weaknesses to build unbreakable loyalty and turn satisfied customers into your most powerful marketing force: brand advocates.

The flaws in corporate customer service (and how to exploit them)

Think about your own experiences dealing with large companies. What frustrations frequently arise? Long hold times listening to repetitive music? Navigating complex phone menus only to be transferred multiple times? Speaking with agents who sound scripted and lack empathy or empowerment to solve your actual problem? Getting lost in automated chatbot loops that lead nowhere? These aren't isolated incidents; they are often systemic flaws inherent in large-scale operations focused on cost-cutting and standardization over genuine connection.

These common corporate failings create massive opportunities for you:

1. **Impersonality vs. Personal Touch:**

   o *Corporate Flaw:* Customers are often treated as numbers in a system. Interactions lack personalization, recognition of past history, or genuine human warmth. Agents may follow rigid scripts.

   o *Your Opportunity:* You can know your customers by name, remember their preferences, reference past conversations, and interact with authentic personality.

You can offer a truly human touch that builds rapport and makes customers feel valued as individuals.

2. **Slow Response Times vs. Agility:**

   o *Corporate Flaw:* Layers of bureaucracy, overloaded support centers, and inefficient processes often lead to frustratingly slow responses to inquiries, complaints, or feedback.

   o *Your Opportunity:* With fewer layers and direct lines of communication, you can respond significantly faster. Quick, helpful responses demonstrate efficiency and respect for the customer's time, creating immediate positive impressions.

3. **Rigid Policies vs. Flexibility:**

   o *Corporate Flaw:* Large companies often have inflexible policies and agents lack the authority to make exceptions or find creative solutions, leading to "computer says no" scenarios.

   o *Your Opportunity:* You have the flexibility to bend the rules (within reason) when appropriate, offer tailored solutions, and empower yourself or your small team to resolve issues effectively and empathetically, turning potential problems into loyalty-building moments.

4. **Reactive Support vs. Proactive Engagement:**

   o *Corporate Flaw:* Support is often purely reactive, only kicking in when a customer actively reports a problem. There's little effort to anticipate needs or check in proactively.

   o *Your Opportunity:* You can proactively reach out to customers – checking if they're happy with their purchase, offering tips related to your product/service, or anticipating potential issues based on their usage patterns. This demonstrates care beyond the point of sale.

5. **Difficulty Reaching Real Humans vs. Accessibility:**

   o *Corporate Flaw:* Customers often face barriers trying to reach a knowledgeable human being, navigating complex IVR systems or unhelpful chatbots.

- ○ *Your Opportunity:* You can make it incredibly easy for customers to connect with a real person who can genuinely help – via clear contact information, responsive email, live chat staffed by knowledgeable individuals, or even direct phone access.

By consciously designing your customer interactions to be the *opposite* of these common corporate frustrations, you don't just provide good service; you create a starkly positive contrast that makes choosing your business feel like a breath of fresh air.

Personalization and engagement tactics to win customer loyalty

Winning loyalty isn't about grand, expensive gestures; it's often about consistent, thoughtful actions that show you genuinely care and understand your customers as individuals. Here are actionable tactics perfectly suited for smaller, agile businesses:

- **Personalized Onboarding (Where Applicable):** If your product/service requires setup or learning, create a tailored onboarding experience. Send personalized welcome emails, offer brief one-on-one setup calls, or create specific tutorial paths based on their stated goals. Ensure they achieve initial success quickly.

- **Remember the Details:** Use a simple CRM (Customer Relationship Management) system – even a well-organized spreadsheet can work initially – to track customer interactions, preferences, past purchases, and even small personal details they might share (like a birthday, a specific project they mentioned). Referencing these details in future interactions shows you're paying attention. ("Hope that project you mentioned last month went well!")

- **Proactive Check-ins:** Don't wait for problems. Reach out occasionally (without being intrusive) after a purchase to see how things are going, offer helpful tips, or share relevant content. A simple, "Just checking in to see if you're loving your [product]?" can go a long way.

- **Handwritten Notes:** In a digital world, a simple, handwritten thank-you note included with an order or sent after a significant interaction stands out dramatically. It takes minimal time but conveys significant care and personal effort. Giants *cannot* replicate this authentically at scale.

- **Segmented Email Marketing:** Go beyond generic email blasts. Segment your list based on purchase history, interests, or engagement level. Send targeted emails with relevant content, personalized recommendations, or special offers tailored to each segment.

- **Exclusive Content or Early Access:** Reward loyal customers with access to exclusive content (behind-the-scenes looks, advanced tips, Q&A sessions with you) or early access to new products/features. This makes them feel like valued insiders.

- **Active Social Media Engagement:** Don't just broadcast; interact. Respond quickly and personally to comments and messages. Ask questions, run polls related to their interests, feature user-generated content, and participate genuinely in conversations within your niche communities.

- **Feedback Loops & Implementation:** Actively solicit feedback through surveys or direct requests. Crucially, acknowledge the feedback and, where feasible, *show* customers you're acting on it. Announce changes made based on customer suggestions. People love feeling heard and seeing their input make a difference.

- **Surprise and Delight:** Occasionally, create unexpected positive moments. Upgrade shipping for free, include a small, unexpected sample or gift with an order, offer a spontaneous loyalty discount, or highlight a customer's success story (with permission). These moments generate significant goodwill and positive word-of-mouth.

The key is authenticity and consistency. These tactics shouldn't feel like manipulative tricks but genuine expressions of appreciation and commitment to your customers' success and satisfaction.

Strategies for making customers your biggest advocates

The pinnacle of customer loyalty isn't just repeat business; it's **advocacy**. Advocates are customers who are so thrilled with your brand and experience that they actively and voluntarily promote you to their networks. They become your unpaid, highly credible sales force. Here's how to cultivate them:

1. **Exceed Expectations Consistently:** Advocacy starts with consistently

delivering exceptional value and service (using the tactics above). You need to reliably go beyond the basics.

2. **Make it Easy to Share:**

    o **Referral Programs:** Implement a simple, rewarding referral program that incentivizes existing customers to bring in new ones (e.g., offer discounts or credits for both the referrer and the referred).

    o **Review Requests:** Politely ask satisfied customers to leave reviews on relevant platforms (Google, Amazon, industry-specific sites). Make it easy by providing direct links. Time these requests strategically after a positive experience or milestone.

    o **Social Sharing Prompts:** Encourage sharing of positive experiences or user-generated content on social media. Create shareable graphics or run contests that involve tagging your brand.

3. **Build a Strong Community:** As mentioned before, a thriving community (Facebook group, forum, etc.) naturally fosters advocacy. Members often answer

questions for prospects, share positive experiences, and defend the brand against criticism. Nurture this space actively.

4. **Showcase Customer Success:** Feature customer testimonials, case studies, and user-generated content prominently on your website and marketing materials. This not only provides social proof but also makes your existing customers feel recognized and valued, reinforcing their loyalty and encouraging others to share.

5. **Engage with Advocates Publicly:** When customers praise you online (reviews, social media), acknowledge and thank them publicly. Amplify their positive messages by sharing or retweeting. This encourages further advocacy.

6. **Create an "Insider" or Ambassador Program:** For your most passionate and engaged customers, consider creating a formal ambassador program offering exclusive perks, early access, direct input on product development, and recognition in exchange for actively promoting the brand.

7. **Empower Them with Information:** Provide advocates with shareable content, talking points, or early insights into upcoming releases so they feel equipped and informed when talking about your brand.

Turning customers into advocates requires nurturing relationships beyond the point of sale. It's about making them feel like valued partners in your brand's journey. Their authentic enthusiasm is far more persuasive than any corporate advertising campaign.

Self-Reflection Questions:

- On a scale of 1-10, how would I rate my current customer service compared to my large competitors? Where are the biggest gaps?

- What is one specific personalization tactic I can implement this week to make my customers feel more individually valued?

- How easy is it currently for my satisfied customers to refer others or leave reviews? How can I simplify this process?

- Am I actively soliciting and acting upon customer feedback? How can I improve this feedback loop?

- What steps can I take to build a stronger sense of community around my brand?

- Are there any "surprise and delight" opportunities I could incorporate into my customer journey?

In the battle against giants, exceptional, personalized customer engagement isn't just a "nice-to-have"; it's a strategic imperative. It's how you build a loyal tribe, insulate yourself from price wars, and create a sustainable competitive advantage that is incredibly difficult for large, impersonal corporations to replicate.

Become a customer magnet, and you'll find your edge sharpens considerably.

Part 3

Tactical Strategies to Outperform Big Competitors

Chapter 6: Winning with SEO & Content Strategy

Search Engine Optimization (SEO) and Content Strategy are not just marketing buzzwords; they are critical battlegrounds where smaller, agile businesses can strategically outmaneuver even the most resource-rich giants. Why? Because success here isn't solely dependent on massive budgets. It rewards **relevance, authority, quality, and a deep understanding of user intent** – areas where focused, niche businesses can often excel. While big brands might dominate broad, high-volume keywords through sheer domain authority and budget, you can win by being smarter, more targeted, and delivering exceptional value within your chosen territory.

This chapter delves into how to craft an SEO and content strategy that punches far above its weight, enabling you to climb the search rankings, attract highly qualified organic traffic, and establish your brand as the go-to resource for your micro-niche.

How to rank higher than big brands with smarter SEO

Trying to outrank Amazon for "buy shoes online" is likely a losing battle. But ranking higher than big brands for specific, niche-focused terms that *your* ideal customers are actually searching for?

That's entirely achievable with a shrewd SEO approach.

- **The Power of Long-Tail Keywords:** This is your secret weapon.

  - **What are they?** Long-tail keywords are longer, more specific search phrases (typically 3+ words) that users type into search engines when they are closer to making a purchase or seeking a very specific solution. Examples: "best waterproof hiking boots for wide feet women" (long-tail) vs. "hiking boots" (head term).

  - **Why they matter for you:**

    - *Lower Competition:* Far fewer websites compete for these specific phrases compared to broad head terms, making it easier for you to rank.

    - *Higher Conversion Intent:* Users searching with long-tail keywords usually have a clearer idea of what they want and are often further along in the buying cycle. Traffic from these terms tends to convert better.

- *Niche Relevance:* They perfectly align with your micro-niche strategy (Chapter 3), allowing you to attract exactly the right audience.

○ **How to Find Them:**

- *Brainstorm:* Think like your customer. What specific questions would they ask? What detailed problems are they trying to solve?

- *Google Autocomplete & "People Also Ask":* Start typing relevant phrases into Google and see what suggestions appear. Look at the "People Also Ask" boxes for related questions.

- *Analyze Competitor Content (Deeply):* What specific topics and sub-topics do your competitors cover in their blog posts or product descriptions? Look for more specific angles they might have missed.

- *Use SEO Tools:* Tools like SEMrush, Ahrefs, Moz Keyword Explorer, or even free tools like Google Keyword Planner allow you to input seed keywords and discover related long-tail variations, along with search volume and difficulty scores. Filter for longer phrases with lower difficulty.

- *Mine Your Own Customer Data:* What language do your customers use in emails, support chats, or reviews? Their natural language often reveals valuable long-tail keywords.

- **Building Topical Authority with Content Clusters & Pillar Pages:** Google increasingly favors websites that demonstrate deep expertise and authority on specific topics. You can achieve this, even against sites with higher overall Domain Authority, by structuring your content intelligently:

  - **Pillar Page:** This is a comprehensive, long-form piece

of content covering a broad core topic central to your niche (e.g., "The Ultimate Guide to Keto Baking for Beginners"). It acts as the central hub.

o **Cluster Content:** These are multiple, shorter pieces of content (blog posts, articles, videos) that delve into specific sub-topics related to the pillar page (e.g., "Best Keto Flours Compared," "Troubleshooting Common Keto Bread Mistakes," "Recipe: Low-Carb Chocolate Chip Cookies").

o **Internal Linking:** Crucially, all cluster content pieces link *back* to the main pillar page, and the pillar page links *out* to the relevant cluster pages. This structure signals to Google that you have extensive coverage of the topic, boosting the authority (and ranking potential) of all pages within the cluster. Ahrefs has a great guide on this topic model: https://ahrefs.com/blog/pillar-pages/

o **Your Advantage:** Big corporate sites often have disorganized content structures. By meticulously building out topic clusters around your core niche areas, you demonstrate focused expertise that Google rewards.

- **On-Page SEO Excellence – Mastering the Fundamentals:** This is where diligence pays off. Smaller businesses can often execute on-page optimization more consistently and meticulously across their focused content portfolio than large organizations managing thousands of pages. Nail these elements for every important page:

  - o **Keyword Integration:** Naturally weave your target keyword (especially long-tail variations) and related semantic terms into your Page Title, Meta Description, Headers (H1, H2, H3), body copy, image alt text, and URL slug. Focus on readability and user intent, not keyword stuffing.

  - o **Compelling Titles & Meta Descriptions:** These are your sales pitch in the search results. Make them clear, benefit-driven, include your keyword, and entice users to click. Optimize length (Titles < 60 chars, Metas ~155-160 chars). A higher Click-

Through Rate (CTR) can positively influence rankings.

o **Clear Content Structure:** Use header tags (H1-H6) logically to break up content, improve readability, and help search engines understand the hierarchy of information. Use short paragraphs, bullet points, and bold text for scan ability.

o **Internal Linking:** Strategically link relevant pages on your site together to distribute authority and guide users (and search engines) to related content.

o **Image Optimization:** Use descriptive file names and informative alt text for all images, incorporating keywords where relevant. This helps with image search and accessibility.

o **User Experience (UX) Signals:** Google considers user experience. Ensure your site is mobile-friendly (responsive design), loads quickly (optimize images, use good hosting, leverage caching), and is easy to navigate. High bounce rates or low time-on-page can signal poor quality. Tools like Google Page Speed Insights can help identify issues.

- **Leveraging Local SEO (If Applicable):** If your business serves a specific geographic area, dominating local search is crucial and often easier than competing nationally.

  - *Google Business Profile (GBP):* Optimize your GBP listing completely and accurately (NAP consistency - Name, Address, Phone), gather positive reviews, upload photos, and use GBP Posts.

  - *Local Keywords:* Target keywords that include location modifiers (e.g., "best keto bakery near downtown Seattle").

  - *Local Citations:* Get listed in relevant online directories (Yelp, industry-specific directories) with consistent NAP information.

  - *Local Content:* Create content relevant to your local audience (e.g., "Guide to Gluten-Free Dining in [Your City]").

Crafting content that Google AND users love

SEO gets users *to* your page, but compelling content keeps them there, converts them, and earns valuable signals (like backlinks and social shares) that further boost your rankings. Your content strategy must be laser-focused on providing exceptional value to your micro-niche.

- **Prioritize Value Over Volume:** Don't try to match the sheer output of large content teams. Instead, focus on creating *better*, more in-depth, more insightful, or more uniquely angled content than anyone else on the specific topics crucial to your niche. One outstanding pillar piece can outperform ten mediocre blog posts. Answer user questions more thoroughly than competitors.

- **Address the Entire Customer Journey:** Create content tailored to different stages of awareness and decision-making:

  - *Top of Funnel (Awareness):* Educational blog posts, guides, infographics addressing broader problems or questions your niche faces. (e.g., "What is Keto Flu and How to Avoid It?")

  - *Middle of Funnel (Consideration):* Comparison guides, case studies, webinars, detailed product reviews helping users evaluate solutions. (e.g., "Comparing Almond Flour vs. Coconut Flour for Keto Baking," "Case Study: How [Customer] Achieved [Result] with Our Service").

- *Bottom of Funnel (Decision):* Highly specific product/service pages, testimonials, free trials/demos, FAQs focused on overcoming final purchase barriers. (e.g., Detailed product page for your Keto Bakers Box, Video testimonials).

- **Embrace Diverse Content Formats:** Don't just rely on text. Engage users and stand out by incorporating:

  - *Video:* Tutorials, product demonstrations, interviews, behind-the-scenes looks.

  - *Infographics:* Visually compelling summaries of data or processes.

  - *Podcasts:* Interviews with experts, deep dives into niche topics.

  - *Interactive Tools:* Calculators, quizzes, configurators relevant to your niche.

- *High-Quality Images:* Original photography or well-designed graphics.
  Big companies might stick to standard formats; your creativity here is an advantage.

- **Inject Your Authentic Brand Voice & Personality:** Remember your position (Chapter 4). Let your unique brand voice shine through. Are you witty? Empathetic? Authoritative? Technical? Consistent voice builds connection and differentiates you from bland, corporate-speak. Tell stories, share your "why," be human.

- **Strategic Content Promotion:** Creating amazing content isn't enough; you need to get eyes on it.

  - *Email List:* Share new content with your subscribers.

  - *Social Media:* Promote strategically on the platforms where your niche hangs out. Tailor the message for each platform.

  - *Online Communities:* Share genuinely helpful content (don't just spam links) in relevant forums, Facebook groups, or Reddit subs.

- Outreach (Carefully): Reach out to relevant bloggers, influencers, or websites who might find your content valuable enough to link to or share (focus on building relationships).

The Symbiotic Relationship:

SEO and Content Marketing are two sides of the same coin. Your keyword research should inform your content topics. Your amazing content should be meticulously optimized for search engines. High-quality content naturally attracts links and social signals, boosting SEO. It's a continuous feedback loop where excellence in one area amplifies success in the other.

Self-Reflection Questions:

- Am I currently targeting specific long-tail keywords relevant to my micro-niche, or am I aiming too broad?

- Is my website content structured logically using pillar pages and topic clusters to demonstrate authority?

- How meticulous is my on-page SEO for my key content pieces and product/service pages? Where can I improve?

- Is my content truly providing superior value and unique insights compared to my competitors, or is it just adding to the noise?

- Am I diversifying my content formats beyond just blog posts?

- What is my strategy for promoting my content after it's published?

By implementing a smart, focused SEO strategy centered around long-tail keywords and topical authority, coupled with creating genuinely valuable, well-optimized content tailored to your micro-niche, you can systematically climb the search rankings and attract a steady stream of ideal customers – often right under the noses of your larger, less focused competitors. This is how you win the visibility battle.

Chapter 7: Marketing That Works (Without a Huge Budget)

You see their ads everywhere. Polished commercials, ubiquitous social media campaigns, sponsored content blanketing the web. Your large competitors seem to operate with marketing budgets that could fund a small nation. How can you possibly compete when your own marketing resources feel more like pocket change in comparison? It's easy to feel discouraged, to believe that visibility is purely a pay-to-play game you're destined to lose.

Throw that belief out the window. While a hefty budget certainly doesn't hurt, it's far from the only path to marketing success, especially online. In fact, relying solely on massive ad spends often breeds complacency and inefficiency in large corporations. Their campaigns can become generic, their targeting sloppy, and their connection with the audience superficial.

This is where you, the agile, focused entrepreneur, find your edge. Marketing without a huge budget forces **creativity, resourcefulness, and a relentless focus on Return on Investment (ROI).** It compels you to be smarter, more targeted, and more engaging. This chapter explores powerful, cost-effective marketing strategies – from guerrilla tactics and viral loops to savvy social media engagement and maximizing free traffic sources – enabling you to generate significant buzz and attract customers without breaking the bank. Think about precision strikes, not carpet bombing.

Leveraging viral growth hacks and guerrilla marketing

Guerrilla marketing isn't about dressing up in a cheap costume (though sometimes creativity takes weird turns!); it's about using unconventional, low-cost tactics to generate buzz, capture attention, and often encourage sharing. Viral growth relies on creating something so inherently interesting, valuable, or emotionally resonant that people *want* to share it, creating exponential reach organically. Here's how to apply these concepts online:

- **Engineer Shareability:** When creating content, products, or campaigns, constantly ask: "Why would someone share this?" Does it make them look smart? Is it funny? Is it incredibly useful? Does it evoke strong emotion (joy, surprise, empathy)? Does it tap into a shared identity or belief within your niche? Building shareability from the beginning is key.

- **Incentivized Referral Programs (with Viral Loops):** Go beyond simple referral discounts. Create programs where *both* the referrer and the referred friend get a significant benefit, and potentially offer tiered rewards for multiple referrals. Consider implementing systems where sharing is easy and integrated into the user experience (e.g., Dropbox's early growth model offering free storage for referrals). Find simple referral program tools online – many offers free or low-cost starting plans.

- **Contests & Giveaways (Done Right):** Simple giveaways can generate quick buzz. To maximize impact:
    - Make the prize highly desirable *specifically to your niche.*
    - Require actions that boost reach (e.g., tag a friend who'd love this, share this post, follow our page). Keep entry simple.
    - Use tools like Gleam or Rafflecopter to manage entries and sharing actions.
    - Ensure compliance with platform rules (e.g., Facebook/Instagram contest guidelines).

- **User-Generated Content (UGC) Campaigns:** Encourage your customers to create content featuring your product or service (photos, videos, testimonials). Run contests for the best UGC, create a dedicated hashtag, and feature customer content prominently on your site and social media. UGC is authentic social proof and free marketing content rolled into one. It shows real people loving your brand.

- **Strategic Piggybacking:** Tap into relevant trending topics, events, or memes *if* you can do so authentically and cleverly, relating it back to your brand or niche without seeming forced or inappropriate. A witty tweet or timely piece of content can gain significant traction. Monitor trends using Google Trends or social media listening.

- **Creative "Online" PR Stunts:** Think outside the box. Could you create a surprisingly useful free tool related to your niche? Launch a quirky side-project that generates attention? Conduct a small, interesting survey within your niche and publish the results? Partner with a complementary brand for an unexpected collaboration? The goal is to generate conversation and earned media attention.

- **Offline-to-Online Guerrilla (If Applicable):** Even for online businesses, clever offline tactics can drive online buzz. Unique stickers, creatively placed flyers with QR codes, or participating in local niche events can generate curiosity and drive website traffic.

Guerrilla and viral tactics often require more creative brainpower than financial investment. They thrive on understanding your audience's psychology and leveraging existing platforms in novel ways.

Smarter social media tactics that outperform paid ads

Big brands often use social media as a one-way broadcast channel, pushing polished ads and corporate messaging. You can win by treating it as a two-way conversation and community-building tool.

- **Deep Engagement Over Broadcasting:** Don't just post and run. Spend significant time *listening* and *engaging*. Respond to every comment and message promptly and personally. Ask questions to spark conversation. Participate in relevant discussions in niche groups or under relevant hashtags (add value, don't just self-promote). Thank people for sharing your content.

- **Niche Platform Domination:** Instead of having a mediocre presence everywhere, identify the 1-2 platforms where your micro-niche is *most* active and engaged (Is it a specific Reddit sub? A dedicated Facebook group? LinkedIn? Instagram? TikTok? Discord?). Go deep on those platforms, become a recognized and valued member of that specific online community.

- **Authenticity Trumps Polish:** While professionalism matters, don't be afraid to show the human side of your brand. Share behind-the-scenes glimpses, introduce yourself or your team, talk about challenges and learnings (vulnerability can build connection), and use an authentic voice, not corporate jargon. People connect with people.

- **Leverage Micro-Influencers:** Forget expensive mega-influencers. Identify micro-influencers (typically 1k-100k followers) who have a smaller but highly engaged and trusting audience *specifically within your niche*. Their recommendations often carry more weight and are significantly more affordable (sometimes collaborations can be product-based rather than cash). Use tools or manual research to find influencers whose audience perfectly matches yours. Check out platforms like Upfluence or AspireIQ for finding relevant influencers.

- **User-Generated Content Curation:** Actively find and re-share positive content your customers post about you (with permission/credit). This validates your brand, provides social proof, and encourages more UGC.

- **Run Engaging Polls & Q&As:** Use platform features like Instagram Stories polls, quizzes, or "Ask Me Anything" sessions (live or pre-recorded) to interact directly with your audience, gather feedback, and provide value in an engaging format.

- **Strategic Use of Video (Low-Budget Friendly):** You don't need a Hollywood studio. Use your smartphone to create simple, authentic videos: quick tips, product demos, answering FAQs, behind-the-scenes tours. Live videos can be particularly engaging and requires minimal editing.

The goal is to build relationships and community, not just collect vanity metrics. Genuine engagement often leads to far greater loyalty and word-of-mouth referrals than expensive, impersonal ad campaigns.

Maximizing free traffic sources

While paid ads offer speed and scale, building sustainable free traffic sources is crucial for long-term, cost-effective growth.

- **SEO & Content Marketing (Foundation - Chapter 6):** This remains paramount. Consistently creating high-value, optimized content targeting relevant long-tail keywords is the most powerful way to attract sustainable, free organic traffic from search engines like Google. Don't neglect this!

- **Email Marketing: Your Owned Asset:** Your email list is one of your most valuable marketing assets – you own the connection, unlike social media followers.

  - *Build Your List:* Offer a compelling lead magnet (free guide, checklist, discount, webinar) in exchange for email sign-ups. Make opt-in forms visible on your website.

  - *Nurture, Don't Just Sell:* Provide consistent value through your emails (tips, insights, exclusive content). Follow the 80/20 rule

(80% value, 20% promotion) or similar.

- o *Segmentation:* Segment your list based on interests or purchase history to send more relevant messages. Even basic segmentation improves results.

- o *Automation (Basic):* Set up simple automated sequences like a welcome series for new subscribers. Many email marketing platforms (like Mailchimp, ConvertKit, Sendinblue) offer free or affordable starting plans. Email marketing consistently delivers one of the highest ROIs of any marketing channel. Check out Campaign Monitor's insights on email marketing ROI: https://www.campaignmonitor.co m/resources/guides/email-marketing-roi/

- **Active Community Participation:** Identify online forums, Facebook groups, LinkedIn groups, Reddit subreddits, Quora topics, or Discord servers where your target audience gathers. Participate *authentically* – answer questions, share expertise, offer help. Build a reputation as a valuable member. Include a link to your website in your profile and only share links to your content when genuinely relevant and helpful (check group rules!).

- **Guest Blogging & Podcast Appearances:** Identify relevant blogs or podcasts in your niche that accept guest contributions or interviews. Prepare a strong pitch offering unique value to *their* audience. This exposes your brand to a new, relevant audience and often provides valuable backlinks for SEO.

- **Basic Public Relations (PR) / HARO:** Sign up for services like Help A Reporter Out (HARO) (https://www.helpareporter.com/). Journalists and bloggers use HARO to find sources for articles. Respond quickly and insightfully to relevant queries. Getting quoted in even small online publications can drive traffic, build credibility, and provide backlinks.

- **Strategic Partnerships & Collaborations:** Partner with non-competing businesses that serve the same or a similar niche audience. Cross-promote each other's content, run joint webinars or giveaways, bundle products, or offer reciprocal discounts. This leverages each other's audiences for mutual benefit.

The Mindset of Lean Marketing:

Marketing without a huge budget requires a specific mindset:

- **Test Everything:** Don't assume what will work. Run small, low-cost experiments for different tactics.

- **Track Your Results:** Use basic analytics (Google Analytics, social media insights, email platform reports) to understand what's working and what's not. Track website traffic sources, conversion rates, and engagement metrics.

- **Focus on ROI:** Pour your limited resources into the channels and tactics that deliver the best measurable results for *your* business.

- **Be Patient & Persistent:** Building organic reach takes time and consistent effort. Don't get discouraged by slow initial results. Keep providing value and refining your approach.

Self-Reflection Questions:

- What is one unconventional or "guerrilla" marketing idea I could test for my business this quarter?

- How much time am I currently spending on genuine social media *engagement* versus just posting content?

- Which 1-2 social media platforms are most crucial for my specific niche, and am I maximizing my presence there?

- What value can I offer to build my email list more effectively?

- Which free traffic sources (SEO, email, communities, guest posting, PR, partnerships) hold the most untapped potential for my business right now?

- Am I effectively tracking the results of my marketing efforts to understand what drives ROI?

Competing against marketing giants isn't about matching their spending dollar for dollar. It's about being smarter, more creative, more targeted, and more focused on building genuine connections and providing exceptional value. By leveraging these cost-effective strategies, you can generate significant momentum, attract your ideal customers, and prove that ingenuity can indeed outperform enormous budgets.

Chapter 8: Speed vs. Size – Moving Faster Than Giants

In the competitive landscape of online business, size often equates to inertia. Large corporations, like massive ocean liners, possess immense power but struggle to change course quickly. They are weighed down by bureaucracy, complex hierarchies, legacy systems, and a deep-seated fear of disrupting established revenue streams. This inherent sluggishness is one of their greatest vulnerabilities, and conversely, one of **your greatest competitive advantages.**

While you may not have their resources, you possess something far more valuable in today's rapidly evolving digital world: **speed and agility.** You can pivot, adapt, experiment, and implement changes at a pace that leaves larger competitors struggling to keep up. This chapter focuses on how to consciously leverage your speed advantage – embracing lean principles, rapid iteration, and swift execution to consistently outmaneuver the giants in your industry.

Why big companies are slow and how to exploit it

Understanding *why* large companies move slowly helps you identify specific opportunities to exploit:

1. **Layers of Decision-Making:** In large organizations, decisions often need approval from multiple departments, committees, and levels of management. Getting a simple idea green-lit can take weeks or months.

   o **Your Edge:** You (or your small, empowered team) can make critical decisions almost instantly. See an opportunity? Seize it. Need to change strategy? Do it. This allows you to react to market shifts or customer feedback in real-time.

2. **Fear of Cannibalization/Risk Aversion:** Established companies are often hesitant to launch innovative products or adopt new business models that might threaten their existing cash cows, even if those innovations represent the future.

   o **Your Edge:** You have less baggage and less to lose. You can embrace disruptive ideas, experiment with novel approaches, and target emerging niches without worrying about upsetting legacy operations. You can be the future while they protect the past.

3. **Complex Internal Processes & Systems:** Integrating new features, updating websites, or launching marketing campaigns in large companies often involves navigating complex internal systems, coordinating multiple teams (IT, marketing, legal, sales), and adhering to rigid protocols.

   - **Your Edge:** You likely have simpler systems and more direct control. You can update your website, launch a new landing page, or start a marketing experiment with far fewer hurdles and dependencies, enabling rapid deployment.

4. **Siloed Departments & Poor Communication:** Information often gets trapped within specific departments in large companies, hindering collaboration and slowing down cross-functional initiatives. Marketing might not know what product development is doing, and

customer service feedback might never reach the right people.

- o **Your Edge:** In a smaller setup, communication is naturally more fluid. Information flows quickly, everyone is likely aware of the broader goals, and feedback loops are shorter, allowing for faster, more informed adjustments.

5. **Focus on Quarterly Results:** Publicly traded companies often prioritize short-term quarterly financial targets, discouraging long-term investments or experiments with uncertain immediate payoffs.

- o **Your Edge:** You can take a longer-term view, investing in strategies (like deep content marketing or community building) that might take time to mature but build sustainable competitive advantages. You can prioritize learning and long-term value creation over immediate, superficial wins.

Exploiting these weaknesses means:

- **Launching Faster:** Bring new products, features, or services to market while competitors are still in committee meetings.

- **Adapting Quicker:** Adjust your offerings, pricing, or marketing based on real-time customer feedback or market shifts while competitors are stuck with annual plans.

- **Experimenting More:** Test new ideas, channels, and tactics rapidly to discover what works, while competitors stick to proven (but potentially outdated) methods.

- **Responding Instantly:** Address customer issues or market opportunities with speed and agility that builds trust and captures fleeting chances.

Lean startup principles for fast execution

The Lean Startup methodology, popularized by Eric Ries, provides a powerful framework for maximizing speed and learning while minimizing wasted resources – perfectly suited for smaller businesses looking to outpace larger rivals. Key principles include:

1. **Build-Measure-Learn Feedback Loop:** Instead of spending months perfecting a

product in isolation, focus on rapidly building a **Minimum Viable Product (MVP)** – the simplest version of your product/service that delivers core value and allows you to start learning.

- o **Build:** Create the MVP quickly.

- o **Measure:** Release it to a small group of early adopters (your niche!) and meticulously measure how they use it and what they say about it (using analytics, surveys, interviews). Focus on actionable metrics, not vanity metrics.

- o **Learn:** Analyze the data and feedback. Did your core assumptions hold true? What needs to change? This learning directly informs the next iteration.

- o **Your Advantage:** Giants often have lengthy development cycles aiming for perfection. You can get real-world feedback and iterate multiple times before they even launch version 1.0. Read more on the Lean Startup methodology here: http://theleanstartup.com/principl es

2. **Validated Learning:** The goal isn't just to build things; it's to learn what customers actually *want* and are willing to pay for. Every product iteration, marketing campaign, or feature launch is an experiment designed to test specific hypotheses about your market. Focus on gaining validated learning about your customers and market with minimal effort.

   o **Your Advantage:** You can afford to be wrong quickly and cheaply. Large companies face significant costs (financial and reputational) if a major launch fails, making them more cautious. Your "failures" are simply learning opportunities that guide you closer to success.

3. **Pivot or Persevere:** Based on your validated learning, make data-driven decisions. If the data shows your current strategy or product isn't working, don't be afraid to **pivot** – make a significant change in direction (e.g., target a different niche, change your core feature set, alter your business model). If the data shows positive signals, **persevere** and continue iterating and optimizing.

   o **Your Advantage:** Pivoting is far easier and less costly for a small, agile business. Giants are often too invested in their current path to make necessary strategic shifts quickly.

Quick testing and iteration methods to outmaneuver competitors

Embracing speed requires practical methods for testing ideas and iterating rapidly:

- **A/B Testing (Split Testing):** Test variations of key elements to see what performs better. This is crucial for optimizing websites, landing pages, email subject lines, ad copy, and calls to action.

  - *Tools:* Google Optimize (free), Optimizely, VWO, Unbounce (for landing pages).

  - *Process:* Change only *one* element at a time (e.g., headline vs. headline, button color vs. button color). Drive sufficient traffic to each variation to get statistically significant results. Implement the winner and test the next element.

  - *Your Advantage:* You can run multiple small, focused A/B tests quickly to continuously improve conversion rates, while large companies might require lengthy processes to approve and implement even simple tests.

- **Landing Page Experiments:** Before investing heavily in building a full product or feature, create a simple landing page describing the concept and include a call to action (e.g., "Sign up for early access," "Register for beta," "Pre-order now"). Drive targeted traffic (e.g., small Google Ads or social media ad spend) to the page. Gauge interest based on conversion rates. If there's little interest, you've saved significant development time and cost.

  - *Tools:* Leadpages, Instapage, Unbounce, Carrd (for simple pages).

- **"Concierge" MVP:** Instead of building complex software or automation initially, manually deliver the core value proposition to your first few customers. For example, if you envision an automated reporting tool, initially create the reports manually for your beta users. This allows you to validate the core value and learn about customer needs *before* writing complex code. You appear high touch while gathering invaluable data.

- **Customer Development Interviews:** Regularly talk directly to your target customers (and potential customers). Don't just pitch your ideas; ask open-ended questions about their problems, workflows, and existing solutions. Use these conversations to validate assumptions, uncover unmet needs, and test reactions to potential features or messaging *before* you build anything. Steve Blank is a key proponent of this: https://steveblank.com/category/customer-development/

- **Rapid Prototyping:** Use tools like Figma, Sketch, or even simple wireframing tools (like Balsamiq) to create clickable prototypes of website flows or app interfaces. Test these prototypes with potential users to get feedback on usability and concept *before* writing code.

- **Agile Project Management:** Adopt agile methodologies (like Scrum or Kanban) even if you're a team of one. Break work into small, manageable tasks (sprints), prioritize ruthlessly, focus on delivering working increments frequently, and hold regular brief check-ins (even with yourself) to review progress and adapt as needed. Tools like Trello, Asana, or Jira can help manage this.

The Culture of Speed:

Leveraging speed isn't just about tools and processes; it's a cultural mindset:

- **Embrace Imperfection:** Don't wait for perfection to launch or test. Get your MVP out there and iterate based on real feedback. "Done is better than perfect" when speed and learning are paramount.

- **Prioritize Ruthlessly:** Focus your limited resources on the activities that deliver the most value and learning *right now*. Use frameworks like the Eisenhower Matrix (Urgent/Important).

- **Empowerment (Even for Yourself):** Give yourself (and your team, if applicable) the authority to make decisions and take action quickly without unnecessary approvals.

- **Fail Fast, Learn Faster:** View setbacks not as failures but as valuable data points. Extract the learnings quickly and apply them to the next iteration.

Self-Reflection Questions:

- Where are the biggest bottlenecks or delays in my current business processes (decision-making, development, marketing execution)?

- Am I currently operating with a "Build-Measure-Learn" mindset, or do I spend too long trying to perfect things before getting feedback?

- What is the simplest version (MVP) of my next product, feature, or marketing idea that I could test quickly?

- How consistently am I using A/B testing or other rapid experimentation methods to optimize my efforts?

- What steps can I take this month to increase the speed and agility of my business operations?

- Am I sometimes held back by a fear of imperfection or failure, preventing me from launching or testing faster?

Your ability to move faster than your larger competitors is a powerful, asymmetric advantage. By embracing lean principles, implementing rapid testing and iteration methods, and cultivating a culture of speed, you can consistently adapt, innovate, and seize opportunities while the giants are still charting their course. Speed isn't just about working harder; it's about working smarter and learning faster.

Part 4

Scaling Without Losing Your Edge

Chapter 9: Automation & Efficiency Hacks

You've found your edge. You're outmaneuvering competitors with speed and smart tactics. Your business is gaining traction, attracting loyal customers, and growing. This is fantastic! But growth brings its own set of challenges. As demand increases, so does the workload. Tasks that were manageable when you were smaller – personally answering every email, manually tracking leads, individually processing orders – can quickly become overwhelming, leading to burnout, decreased quality, and ironically, a loss of the very agility and personal touch that gave you your edge.

The answer isn't necessarily hiring a massive team overnight (which can introduce its own complexities and costs). Instead, the key lies in **strategic automation and ruthless efficiency.** By leveraging the right tools and optimizing your workflows, you can handle increased volume, free up your valuable time for high-impact activities (like strategy, customer relationships, and innovation), and scale your business sustainably without sacrificing quality or your unique advantage. This chapter provides practical automation and efficiency hacks specifically chosen for lean, growing online businesses.

Must-have tools for scaling without burnout

Technology is your ally in efficient scaling. Many powerful tools, once prohibitively expensive, now offer affordable (or even free) starting plans perfect for smaller businesses. Focus on tools that automate repetitive tasks, streamline workflows, and provide valuable insights. Here are key categories and examples:

1. **Email Marketing Automation:** Essential for nurturing leads and engaging customers at scale without manual effort for every email.

   o *Key Features:* List segmentation, automated sequences (welcome series, abandoned cart recovery, post-purchase follow-ups), visual workflow builders, analytics.

   o *Tools:* Mailchimp, ConvertKit, ActiveCampaign, Sendinblue, MailerLite. (Choose based on your specific needs and budget – some are better for e-commerce, others for creators, etc.)

2. **Social Media Management & Scheduling:** Manage multiple profiles, schedule posts in advance, and monitor engagement from one dashboard.

   - *Key Features:* Content scheduling across platforms, social listening (monitoring mentions), engagement tracking, analytics reporting.

   - *Tools:* Buffer, Hootsuite, Later (especially good for visual platforms like Instagram), Agorapulse, Sprout Social (more enterprise-focused but powerful).

3. **Customer Relationship Management (CRM):** Organize customer data, track interactions, manage sales pipelines, and personalize communication. Essential for maintaining relationships as you grow.

   - *Key Features:* Contact management, deal tracking, communication history logging, task management, basic automation (e.g., follow-up reminders).

   - *Tools:* HubSpot CRM (offers a robust free tier), Zoho CRM, Pipedrive, Insightly, Freshsales.

Even a well-structured tool like Airtable can function as a simple CRM initially.

4. **Project Management & Collaboration:** Keep tasks organized, track progress, and collaborate effectively (even if it's just managing your own workload or working with freelancers).

   - *Key Features:* Task creation & assignment, deadlines, progress tracking (Kanban boards, lists, calendars), file sharing, communication threads.

   - *Tools:* Trello (simple Kanban), Asana (more feature-rich), Monday.com, ClickUp, Notion (highly flexible workspace).

5. **Customer Support & Help Desk Software:** Manage customer inquiries efficiently, track support tickets, and build a knowledge base to enable self-service.

   - *Key Features:* Ticket management system, shared inbox, knowledge base builder, canned responses, basic automation rules, reporting.

   - *Tools:* Help Scout, Zendesk, Freshdesk, Gorgias (popular for e-commerce), Intercom (strong on chat and engagement). Many offer free or low-cost plans.

6. **Workflow Automation (Connecting Apps):** Automate tasks *between* different applications without writing code. This is incredibly powerful for eliminating manual data entry and connecting disparate systems.

   o *Key Features:* Trigger-action workflows (e.g., "When new order in Shopify [Trigger], add customer to Mailchimp list [Action]"). Huge library of app integrations.

   o *Tools:* Zapier (market leader, extensive integrations), Make (formerly Integromat - powerful visual builder), IFTTT (simpler, often free).

7. **Analytics & Reporting:** Understand website traffic, user behavior, marketing campaign performance, and sales data to make informed decisions.

   o *Key Features:* Traffic analysis, conversion tracking, audience insights, custom report building.

   o *Tools:* Google Analytics (essential & free), Google Search Console (essential & free), platform-specific analytics (e.g., Shopify Analytics, social media insights), Hotjar (heatmaps & session recordings to understand user behavior).

Choosing Tools Wisely:

- **Start Simple:** Don't try to implement everything at once. Identify your biggest time-sinks or bottlenecks and find a tool to address *that specific problem* first.

- **Focus on Integration:** Choose tools that can integrate with each other (directly or via Zapier/Make) to create seamless workflows.

- **Consider Scalability:** Opt for tools that offer tiered pricing, allowing you to upgrade features as your needs grow.

- **Prioritize User-Friendliness:** A complex tool you never learn to use properly is useless. Choose interfaces you find intuitive.

The right way to automate without losing the personal touch

Automation is powerful, but misused, it can create the same impersonal experience you're trying to avoid. The goal is to automate the *repetitive* and *impersonal*, freeing up *your* time for the *personal* and *high-value* interactions.

- **Automate Processes, Not Relationships:** Automate tasks like sending order confirmations, scheduling social media posts, tagging customers based on behavior, or generating basic reports. Don't automate genuine relationship-building conversations or responses to complex customer issues where empathy is needed.

- **Use Personalization Tokens Wisely:** Most automation tools allow personalization (e.g., inserting [First Name]). Use them! But ensure your data is clean (no "Dear [blank]") and consider segmenting deeply so the automated message still feels highly relevant.

- **Set Clear Expectations:** If using chatbots for initial support queries, make it clear it's a bot and provide an easy escalation path to a human agent.

- **Segment Ruthlessly:** The more you segment your audience (based on interests, purchase history, engagement), the more relevant and personal your automated messages will feel. A targeted automated email to a small segment feels less like spam and more like helpful communication.

- **Maintain Human Oversight:** Regularly review your automated workflows. Are they performing as expected? Are automated responses appropriate? Is the tone right? Be ready to jump in manually when an automated process isn't sufficient or goes awry.

- **Use Automation to *Enable* Personalization:** Use CRM data and automation to *trigger* personal outreach. For example, set an automated task reminder for yourself to personally email a high-value customer on their one-year anniversary with your brand, rather than sending a generic automated email. Use automation to identify opportunities for human connection.

- **Focus Automation on Internal Efficiency First:** Automate backend processes like data entry between apps, task assignments, or report generation. These efficiency gains free up your time without directly impacting the customer-facing experience, allowing you to spend *more* time on personalized interactions.

Building efficient workflows that free up your time

Beyond specific tools, optimizing your *overall* way of working is crucial for efficiency as you scale.

- **Document Your Processes (SOPs):** Create simple Standard Operating Procedures (SOPs) for recurring tasks (e.g., processing orders, onboarding new clients, publishing blog posts). This ensures consistency (even if it's just you doing it), makes tasks faster, and is essential if you eventually delegate or hire. Use checklists, screen recordings (Loom is great for this), or simple documents.

- **Batch Similar Tasks:** Group similar tasks together and do them in focused blocks (e.g., answer all emails at specific times, schedule all social media posts for the week in one session, process all orders once a day). Constant context-switching kills productivity.

- **Template Everything:** Create templates for frequently sent emails, social media post formats, project briefs, proposals, reports, etc. This saves time and ensures consistency. Store them in an easily accessible place.

- **Prioritize Ruthlessly (Again!):** Use frameworks like the Eisenhower Matrix

(Urgent/Important) or time blocking to focus on high-impact activities. Learn to say "no" to tasks or opportunities that don't align with your core goals. Delegate or eliminate low-value tasks whenever possible.

- **Optimize Your Workspace:** Ensure your physical and digital workspaces are organized and free from distractions. Use browser extensions to block distracting websites during focused work blocks.

- **Continuous Improvement Mindset:** Regularly review your workflows. Ask yourself: "Is there a faster, simpler, or more automated way to do this?" Look for bottlenecks and opportunities for optimization. Even small improvements compound over time.

Self-Reflection Questions:

- What are the top 3-5 most repetitive, time-consuming tasks in my business right now?

- Which software tools could potentially automate or significantly streamline these tasks?

- Where can I implement automation *without* sacrificing the personal touch that differentiates my brand?

- Are my current workflows documented? If not, what is one key process I can document this week?

- How effectively am I batching tasks and managing my time to focus on high-impact activities?

- What is one efficiency hack or tool I can experiment with this month?

Scaling your online business doesn't have to mean succumbing to chaos or losing your unique edge. By strategically implementing automation, leveraging the right tools, and continuously optimizing your workflows, you can handle growth efficiently, free up your invaluable time, and focus your energy where it matters most – delighting your customers, innovating, and staying ahead of the competition. Efficiency isn't just about doing more; it's about creating the space to do what truly matters, better.

Chapter 10: Creating a Brand That Sticks

You've navigated the competitive landscape, carved out your niche, honed your positioning, mastered customer service, implemented smart marketing tactics, leveraged speed, and optimized your efficiency. You've built a business that not only competes but actively thrives by being smarter, faster, and more connected than the giants. But how do you ensure this success isn't fleeting? How do you build something truly enduring, something that customers feel deeply connected to, something that becomes less of a mere product or service and more of an integral part of their lives or identities?

The answer lies in consciously cultivating a **brand that sticks**. This goes beyond clever marketing or excellent service; it delves into the realm of emotional connection, shared identity, and unwavering trust. A sticky brand creates a loyal tribe, fosters genuine emotional resonance, and ultimately turns satisfied customers into passionate, lifelong ambassadors. This deep-seated loyalty becomes your ultimate, almost impenetrable competitive moat — something competitors, especially large, impersonal ones, find incredibly difficult to replicate or erode. This final strategic chapter focuses on solidifying your edge by building a brand with lasting adhesive power.

Building a Loyal Tribe of Customers

Individual customer loyalty is crucial (Chapter 5), but elevating that to a *collective sense of belonging* – a tribe – creates an exponentially more powerful force. A tribe shares an identity, rallies around common values or interests (often centered on your brand), and feels a connection not just to your business, but *to each other.*

- **Reinforce Shared Identity and Values:** Continuously articulate and demonstrate the core values and identity that define your brand and resonate with your micro-niche. Is your tribe about creativity? Sustainability? Peak performance? Minimalist living? Technical mastery? Make this identity explicit in your messaging, content, and actions. Customers should feel, "Yes, these are my people. This brand *gets* me."

- **Create Exclusive Community Spaces:** Provide dedicated platforms where your tribe can connect, share experiences, ask questions, and support each other. This could be:

  o A private Facebook Group or Discord server.

- An exclusive forum on your website.

- Regular virtual meetups or Q&A sessions.

- Niche event sponsorships or participation where your tribe gathers.
  Actively moderate and participate in these spaces, fostering positive interaction and reinforcing the community spirit. The value comes from member-to-member interaction as much as from interaction with your brand.

- **Establish Rituals and Traditions:** Small, consistent brand experiences can build a sense of shared ritual and belonging. This could be anything from:

  - A specific way you package orders.

  - A unique sign-off in your emails.

  - An annual customer appreciation event or sale.

  - Regular content series (e.g., "Technique Tuesday," "Feature Friday").

o A unique unboxing experience. These seemingly small details create familiarity and a sense of shared experience unique to your brand's insiders.

- **Empower Your Members:** Give your tribe a voice and influence. Solicit their input on new product ideas, feature requests, or content topics. Feature member spotlights or user-generated content prominently. Ask for their help in beta testing. When members feel they have a stake in the brand's direction, their loyalty deepens significantly. They transition from passive consumers to active participants.

Building a tribe isn't about trapping people; it's about creating a space so valuable, supportive, and aligned with their identity that they *choose* to belong and actively participate.

How to create emotional connections with your audience

Logic might drive initial consideration, but **emotion drives loyalty and advocacy.** People stick with brands that make them *feel* something – understood, inspired, safe, delighted, empowered, or simply happy. Larger competitors often struggle to forge genuine emotional connections at scale. This is your opportunity to connect on a deeper level.

- **Master Brand Storytelling:** Facts tell, stories sell (and connect). Weave narratives throughout your brand communications:

  - **Origin Story:** Why did you start this business? What personal passion or problem drove its creation? Authenticity is key.

  - **Mission Story:** What impact are you trying to make beyond profit? What future are you trying to build for your customers or your niche?

  - **Customer Stories:** Share relatable stories (case studies, testimonials told as narratives) of how your product/service has positively impacted real people within your tribe. Focus on the transformation, not just the features.

  - **Behind-the-Scenes Stories:** Humanize your brand by sharing glimpses of your process, your team, your challenges, and your successes.

- **Develop an Authentic Voice and Personality:** As discussed before, consistency in your brand voice (witty, empathetic, authoritative, etc.) across all touchpoints builds familiarity and rapport. Let your brand's unique personality shine through. Avoid generic corporate-speak at all costs. Your authentic voice makes your brand feel like a trusted friend rather than a faceless entity.

- **Elevate Surprise and Delight:** Move beyond occasional small gestures (Chapter 5) to create truly memorable, emotionally resonant moments for loyal customers or during critical interactions. This might involve:

  o A highly personalized gift related to their known interests.

  o Going extraordinary lengths to solve a difficult problem.

  o Celebrating major customer milestones in a significant way.

  o Creating exclusive, unexpected experiences.
  These "wow" moments create powerful emotional anchors and generate incredible word-of-mouth.

- **Align with Deeper Values:** Increasingly, consumers want to support brands that align with their personal values (sustainability, ethical sourcing, social justice, community support, etc.). If your brand genuinely holds strong value:

  o Communicate with them clearly and authentically.

  o Demonstrate your commitment through tangible actions and transparency (don't just talk the talk).

  o Attract and retain customers who share those values, creating a powerful bond based on shared principles, not just product utility. This connection often transcends price sensitivity.

Emotional connection transforms customers from transactional buyers into engaged fans who feel invested in your brand's success.

Turning Customers into Lifelong Brand Ambassadors

The ultimate goal is to cultivate customers who are not just loyal but become **lifelong ambassadors** – individuals who proactively and enthusiastically recommend your brand over the long term, becoming a sustainable engine for growth and a powerful defense against competitors.

- **Nurture Your Top Advocates:** Identify your most loyal, engaged, and vocal supporters (through purchase history, community participation, reviews, referrals). Treat them like VIPs:

    o Give them exclusive early access or sneak peeks.

    o Solicit their feedback directly on strategic decisions.

    o Offer personalized rewards or recognition.

    o Build genuine personal relationships where appropriate. Make them feel truly valued and appreciated for their support.

- **Equip Them to Share:** Make it incredibly easy for ambassadors to spread the word:

- Provide them with unique referral codes or shareable links.

- Create easily shareable content (infographics, key stats, compelling video snippets).

- Offer simple talking points or "elevator pitches" about your brand's key differentiators.

- Consider creating an "ambassador kit" (digital or physical) with resources and branded items.

- **Maintain Long-Term Relationship Management:** Don't just focus on the next sale. Stay connected with your loyal customer base over time, even during periods when they aren't actively buying. Continue providing value through content, community engagement, and occasional check-ins. Ensure they continue to feel part of the tribe.

- **Build a Legacy Brand Mindset:** Think beyond short-term wins and quarterly targets. Focus on building a brand known for enduring quality, unwavering integrity, consistent value, and a positive impact on its community or niche. Make decisions that prioritize long-term reputation and customer trust over immediate gains. A brand built with a legacy mindset naturally inspires deeper, more lasting loyalty and advocacy.

Lifelong ambassadors are earned, not bought. They are the natural outcome of consistently delivering exceptional value, fostering genuine connections, building a strong community, and operating with integrity over the long haul.

Self-Reflection Questions:

- Does my brand currently foster a sense of shared identity or community among its customers? How could I strengthen this?

- What is the core emotional connection I want customers to have with my brand? How effectively am I creating that feeling?

- Am I effectively using storytelling (origin, mission, customer) in my brand communications?

- Who are my most loyal customers/potential advocates right now? How am I nurturing those specific relationships?

- What steps can I take to make it easier and more rewarding for satisfied customers to become active brand ambassadors?

- Am I making business decisions with a focus on long-term brand reputation and customer trust?

Creating a brand that sticks is the culmination of all the strategies discussed in this book. It's the ultimate expression of finding your edge – an edge built not just on clever tactics, but on genuine value, authentic connection, and unwavering commitment to the tribe you serve. It's how you move from simply competing to building a truly beloved and enduring online business.

Conclusion: The Roadmap to Long-Term Success

We embarked on this journey together facing a landscape that can often feel intimidating – the vast, turbulent ocean of online business, seemingly dominated by colossal Goliaths casting long shadows. The question loomed large: How can the smaller, agile player possibly hope to compete, let alone win? Throughout the pages of *Finding Your Edge*, we've systematically dismantled the myth of corporate invincibility and illuminated a clear, actionable path forward. It's a path defined not by imitating the giants, nor by retreating in fear, but by strategically **finding, sharpening, and wielding your unique competitive edge.**

This journey wasn't about discovering a magical shortcut or a secret loophole. Instead, it was about embracing a different way of thinking and operating – one that leverages your inherent strengths as a focused, agile, and customer-centric business. We've explored the crucial tactics and mindset shifts required to transform yourself from a potential victim of competition into a formidable, strategic player capable of carving out and dominating your chosen territory.

Key Takeaways and Action Steps: Your Edge Toolkit Recap

Let's quickly revisit the core components of your newly acquired edge toolkit:

1. **Embrace the Underdog Advantage (Chapter 1):** Recognize that size often breeds slowness and impersonality. Your agility, focus, and ability to connect personally are potent weapons.

2. **Master Competitive Intelligence (Chapter 2):** Continuously analyze your competitors – not to copy, but to understand their strengths, pinpoint their weaknesses, and identify the crucial market gaps *you* can fill.

3. **Dominate Through Micro-Niching (Chapter 3):** Avoid direct confrontation in broad markets. Laser-focus on a specific, underserved micro-niche where you can become the undisputed expert and go-to solution.

4. **Position Like a Pro (Chapter 4):** Craft a compelling Unique Selling Proposition (USP) and strategically position your brand in the customer's mind as the distinct, desirable choice for your niche.

5. **Become a Customer Magnet (Chapter 5):** Exploit the service gaps left by large corporations. Deliver exceptional, personalized experiences that foster

deep loyalty and turn customers into vocal advocates.

6. **Win with Smart SEO & Content (Chapter 6):** Leverage long-tail keywords, build topical authority, and create outstanding, value-driven content optimized to attract your ideal audience organically via search engines.

7. **Market Lean and Mean (Chapter 7):** Employ creative, low-cost marketing tactics – guerrilla marketing, viral loops, authentic social engagement, maximizing free traffic sources – to generate buzz and leads without a giant budget.

8. **Weaponize Speed and Agility (Chapter 8):** Use Lean Startup principles, rapid iteration, and swift execution to out-learn and outmaneuver slower-moving competitors. Adaptability is your superpower.

9. **Scale Smart with Automation (Chapter 9):** Implement tools and efficient workflows to handle growth without burnout, automating repetitive tasks to free up your time for high-value, personalized interactions.

10. **Build a Brand That Sticks (Chapter 10):** Cultivate a loyal tribe, forge genuine

emotional connections, and nurture lifelong brand ambassadors through shared identity, consistent value, and authentic storytelling.

This isn't just a collection of isolated tactics; it's an integrated system. Your niche focus informs your positioning. Your positioning guides your content and marketing. Your customer focus fuels your brand loyalty. Your speed enables you to capitalize on opportunities identified through analysis. Each element reinforces the others, creating a powerful, synergistic effect.

Your Immediate Action Roadmap:

Knowledge without action is merely potential energy. To truly find and leverage your edge, implementation is key. Consider these immediate next steps:

1. **Revisit Your Competitive Analysis:** Dedicate time *this week* to review your key competitors using the frameworks and tools discussed. Identify one specific weakness you can start exploiting.

2. **Sharpen Your USP & Positioning:** Can you articulate your USP in one clear, compelling sentence targeted at your micro-niche? Refine it and start weaving it more prominently into your website and marketing.

3. **Identify ONE Micro-Niche Tactic:** Choose one actionable idea from Chapter 3 (e.g., explore a specific sub-group, research relevant long-tail keywords) and begin validating its potential.

4. **Implement ONE Customer Magnet Idea:** Select one tactic from Chapter 5 (e.g., send a personalized follow-up email, start soliciting reviews more actively, plan a small "surprise and delight" initiative) and put it into action.

5. **Optimize ONE Piece of Content:** Choose a key blog post or page. Audit its on-page SEO using the checklist from Chapter 6 and make improvements.

6. **Experiment with ONE Lean Marketing Tactic:** Try a small, low-cost experiment from Chapter 7 (e.g., run a small UGC contest, test a new social media engagement approach, map out a basic email welcome series).

7. **Identify ONE Efficiency Win:** Find one repetitive task you can automate (using Zapier/Make or a dedicated tool) or streamline (by creating a template or SOP) this month, as discussed in Chapter 9.

Don't try to do everything at once. Pick one or two high-impact actions from the areas most relevant to your current challenges and start building momentum. Consistent, focused action is far more effective than sporadic bursts of effort.

How to keep innovating and staying ahead

Finding your edge isn't a one-time event; it's a continuous process of refinement, adaptation, and innovation. The market never stands still. Competitors react. Customer needs evolve. New technologies emerge. To maintain your edge long-term, you must cultivate a mindset of perpetual learning and adaptation:

- **Stay Curious:** Never stop learning about your industry, your customers, emerging technologies, and marketing trends. Read industry blogs, listen to podcasts, attend webinars, and engage with thought leaders. Resources like the HubSpot Marketing Blog (https://blog.hubspot.com/marketing) or MarketingProfs (https://www.marketingprofs.com/) offer a wealth of ongoing insights.

- **Keep Listening:** Maintain those feedback loops with your customers (surveys, interviews, social listening).

Their evolving needs and frustrations are your best source of ideas for innovation.

- **Continue Experimenting:** Never assume you've found the "perfect" formula. Keep running small tests (A/B tests, landing page experiments, marketing channel tests) to continuously optimize and uncover new opportunities.

- **Revisit Your Strategy Regularly:** Periodically (e.g., quarterly or annually), step back and review your niche focus, positioning, competitive landscape, and overall strategy. Are your assumptions still valid? Do adjustments need to be made?

- **Don't Fear Calculated Risks:** While giants are risk-averse, your agility allows you to take calculated risks on new ideas or technologies that could provide the next significant leap forward. For insights into future trends and strategic thinking, exploring resources like Harvard Business Review's Strategy section (https://hbr.org/topic/strategy) can be valuable.

Final Words of Encouragement: Your Edge is Within Reach

The path of the online entrepreneur facing formidable competition is undeniably challenging. There will be moments of doubt, setbacks, and the temptation to compare your journey unfavorably to the seemingly effortless success of larger players.

Remember this: **Your size is not your limitation; it is your launchpad.** Your ability to focus, connect deeply, move quickly, and provide genuine value is an edge that no amount of corporate funding can easily replicate. The strategies and tactics outlined in this book provide the framework, but the ultimate success comes from your dedication, your creativity, and your unwavering commitment to serving your chosen audience exceptionally well.

You don't need to be Goliath to win. You need to be David – strategic, agile, precise, and armed with the right tools. You have the capacity to not just survive in the crowded online marketplace, but to thrive, build a loyal tribe, and create a lasting, impactful business on your own terms.

The edge you seek is not some mythical artifact hidden away; it's forged through deliberate action, continuous learning, and the courage to be different. Go find it. Sharpen it. Wield it. Your thriving online business awaits.